Changing the Game

© RIBA Publishing 2025

Published by RIBA Publishing
66 Portland Place
London W1B 1AD

ISBN 9781 91572 209 6

The rights of Tara Gbolade and Lanre Gbolade to be identified as
the Authors of this Work has been asserted in accordance with
the Copyright, Designs and Patents Act 1988 sections 77 and 78.

All rights reserved. No part of this publication may be reproduced,
stored in a retrieval system, or transmitted, in any form or by any
means, electronic, mechanical, photocopying, recording or otherwise,
without prior permission of the copyright owner.

British Library Cataloguing-in-Publication Data
A catalogue record for this book is available from the British Library.

Commissioning Editor: Clare Holloway/Anna Watson
Publishing coordinator: Patricia Roig
Production: Richard Blackburn
Designed and Typeset by CHK Design
Printed and bound by Bain & Bell, Glasgow
Cover designed by CHK Design

While every effort has been made to check the accuracy and quality
of the information given in this publication, neither the Author
nor the Publisher accept any responsibility for the subsequent use
of this information, for any errors or omissions that it may contain,
or for any misunderstandings arising from it.

www.ribapublishing.com

CHANGING THE GAME

HOW TO BE A SUSTAINABLE AND REGENERATIVE SMALL PRACTICE

TARA GBOLADE
WITH LANRE GBOLADE

RIBA Publishing

DEDICATION

This book is dedicated to all the small practices and businesses operating in the built environment sector who remain committed to pushing boundaries of sustainable practice and project delivery, making the difficult changes our world needs despite our precarious times. We hope this book acts as a stimulus for those beginning their journey towards a regenerative mode of practice and provides continued encouragement for those already on the journey to disrupt the status quo.

ACKNOWLEDGEMENTS 6
PREFACE 7

1
INTRODUCTION
8

2
YOUR PRACTICE
18

3
ENVIRONMENTAL REGENERATION
40

4
SOCIAL SUSTAINABILITY AND ENGAGEMENT
80

5
ECONOMIC SUSTAINABILITY
106

6
CONCLUSION
128

NOTES 133
INDEX 139
IMAGE CREDITS 143

ACKNOWLEDGEMENTS

This book would not have been possible without the mammoth effort made by a host of good humans – it truly is the work of many hands, all of whom we are profoundly grateful to.

We extend our thanks to the contributing practices and their co-founders, who generously shared their invaluable insights and experiences in architectural practice and education. Most run small, busy practices and all of them push boundaries in their field of expertise around environmental, social and economic sustainability. Through interviews, phone calls and impromptu discussions, we collaborated to create case studies, which offer lessons dove-tailing with the themes of each chapter. The detailed insights provided by these contributors, drawn from their experiences in architecture, planning, engagement and running businesses, were instrumental in forming the key principles that have been brought forth in this book. We deeply appreciate all contributors for their dedication to driving change in the industry and challenging the business-as-usual model, and for their support and enthusiasm throughout the development of this book.

We are also grateful to the RIBA Publishing team for their encouragement, support, guidance and patience during the creation of this book. In particular our thanks go to Helen Castle, Publishing Director at RIBA Publishing, for commissioning this important book. We'd like to thank our heroic editors Clare Holloway, who started this journey with us, Anna Watson who brought us to the finish line and Lizzy Silverton from First Pages for her immense patience and ability to source and collate all the images. Our gratitude also extends to the production team, including Richard Blackburn who steered the book to print, and CHK Design for the thoughtful design of the book's graphic layout, and again to Lizzy Silverton – this time with her copy-editing hat on – for meticulously reviewing the final draft.

A special thank you goes to our reviewers who kindly read the manuscript in its early stages and provided supportive and constructive feedback for improvement. These include Barbara Kaucky, Jonathan Hagos and Marianne Davys.

We are immensely grateful to our industry, one that really does seem to be moving forwards in addressing our climate crisis in a collaborative way.

Finally, a heartfelt thank you to our family and friends who encouraged us along the way, and who were gracious about us not spending nearly as much time with them as we should have during the period it took to write this book.

PREFACE

When looking at how small practices can respond to an increasingly complicated working environment, we are repeatedly drawn to the wisdom of those who so eloquently capture the essence of our craft. One such voice is that of Lesley Lokko OBE, who wrote of creating the 'just city', observing that, 'there is a genuine desire to create a more equitable, inclusive, resilient city … but it is a complex, difficult, and, at times, seemingly impossible task'.[1] These words resonate deeply with us as a small architectural practice, as we strive to create buildings, spaces and places that have the ability to enhance the lives of their occupants. In this book, we explore how adopting a regenerative approach to the practice of architecture might encourage a more nuanced intersection of the environmental, social and economic sustainability of the places we shape, and how, in embracing and reframing this complexity, we can design and live a far more enriching life.

Tara Gbolade and Lanre Gbolade
June 2024

INTROD

UCTION

*'For preserving the earth isn't a battle too large
To win, but a blessing too large to lose.
This is the most pressing truth:
That our people have only one planet to call home
And our planet has only one people to call its own.
We can either divide and be conquered by the few,
Or we can decide to conquer the future,
And say that today a new dawn we wrote,
Say that as long as we have humanity,
We will forever have hope.
[...]
I challenge you to heed this call,
I dare you to shape our fate.
Above all, I dare you to do good
So that the
world might be great..'*

— Amanda Gorman, 'An Ode We Owe', poem for the SDG Moment 2022, during the 77th UN General Assembly[1]

Amanda Gorman's poem serves as a poignant call to action, urging society – including we as architects – to acknowledge the impact of our practices on the planet, and to rethink our relationship with our environment. The poem's vivid imagery of a world on the brink serves as a powerful reminder that our role is one of environmental and societal stewardship. Gorman's message is clear: the built environment must reflect our duty to future generations. Heeding her words will require us to embrace our creativity, analytical, practical, and wisdom-based skills and attitudes to defy our learned behaviours and routinised patterns such that we can generate novel and compelling ideas in the face of opposition.

'Changing the game' is a maxim that can be used to imply a significant shift or transformation in our established norms, rules or methods. It suggests an innovative and even disruptive approach that redefines current standards or expectations. These changes often take the form of vast leaps in a particular area, but sometimes, indeed most times, changing the game is a step in an evolutionary process that has already begun. We have found that changing the game often follows a moment that ignites a movement: it is the change to our Building Regulations following the tragic fire at Grenfell Tower in the summer of 2017; it is the rethinking of the participation of diverse voices in society after the murder of George Floyd by police officers in 2020; it is the new Clean Air (Human Rights) Bill, or 'Ella's Law', campaigned for by a mother following the death of her child, and changing our air pollution policies for good. Changing the game is an industry that responds to our climate crisis by forming a grassroots organisation to drive change. Changing the game is a collective of small

Fig 1.1 Amanda Gorman, American poet and activist

architectural practices committing to care about our planet and its people and determining to act before it's too late.

We believe that choosing to become a game changer will drive what a successful small architecture practice looks like in the 21st century. We are living through a period of immense and urgent change: the technological revolution has transformed the way we live and work, and the environment we live in is changing too. Accelerated by our own actions, by an insatiable thirst for growth at all costs, we are living through serious climate and biodiversity emergencies. Our extractive policies over the past centuries have triggered economic, social, ecological and political crises. At the time of writing, we are entering what is deemed to be the deepest recession since the 1930s. Concerns over the escalating price of fuel, the cost-of-living crisis and how we treat immigrants from war-torn countries dominate our headlines. But, being the agents of our own demise, surely, we can be the problem solvers too.

Finding solutions will require a different, more holistic way of thinking. This book takes a radically optimistic view in exploring how we can make the necessary changes to keep our planet within the 1.5°C global temperature rise goal, while at the same time protecting and improving the lives of its people. We explore how small practices can position themselves to ensure that, following the most active decade since the Industrial Revolution, we lead with regenerative principles, resilience and innovation to thrive beyond this decade of change. How can small practices change the game in an industry dominated by a business-as-usual approach? What will a new way of being require from us? What is the cost? And how must we respond?

OUR WORLD TODAY

We live in a world where children born today are seven times more likely to face extreme weather than their grandparents.[2] In the summer of 2022, the UK faced the hottest temperatures ever recorded in the country (40°C), leading to the Met Office's first ever issuance of a red 'extreme heat' warning.[3] Alongside spreading fires, the extreme heat caused huge economic and social upheaval, including 2,985 deaths above those expected for the period.[4] This is a direct result of global warming and an excess of carbon emissions.

Approximately 39% of global energy-related carbon emissions come from our buildings: 28% from operational emissions (the energy used to heat, cool and power them) and 11% from materials and construction.[5] Yet, over the next few decades, cities are set to grow and expand, with urban extensions and intensifications planned across the country through government-led developments, such as garden cities. Public debates question whether our government should build new towns, with arguments in favour citing a need to solve the housing crisis, while those against make a case for densifying existing towns instead. In either event, new construction will continue to happen. Besides the clear dent that the COVID 19 pandemic and the war in the Ukraine has had on construction, our industry continues to grow steadily. The value of construction work in Great Britain has grown over the last 15 years and in 2022 it reached a record high of £132,989 million (see fig. 1.2), driven by both private and public sector work (with the growth in the private sector outstripping the public sector).[6]

CHAPTER 1
INTRODUCTION

Types of construction work, current prices, non-seasonally adjusted, Great Britain, 2010 to 2022. Key:

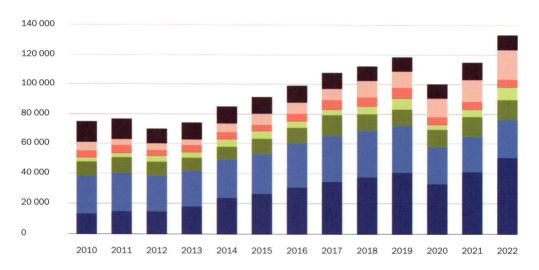

Fig 1.2 Increase in value of construction work in the UK, 2010–22, Construction statistics, Great Britain: 2022 (tables 1.1, 1.2 and 1.3), source: Office for National Statistics

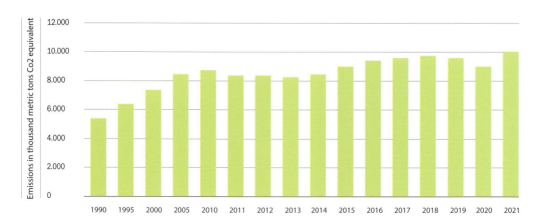

Fig 1.3 Greenhouse gas emissions from buildings and construction activity in the UK remains high, 1990–2020, source: Statista

THE POWER OF SMALL
'If you think you are too small to make a difference, try sleeping in a room with a mosquito.'
— Dalai Lama

While the challenges outlined above are big in scale and impact, we believe that all small practices have a significant role to play in how we address them. Of the 3,630 practices in the UK, 80% are small practices, employing between one and 10 members of staff, and, of them, 41% employ just one or two people.[7] While we might be small in size, here before us stands a unique opportunity to change the narrative. We are not just architects. We are passionate place-makers. Optimistic in our thinking and entrepreneurial in our actions, we can play our part in making the everyday extraordinary through our practice.

An exasperated public are on our side too. They have called on us to change our policies on climate adaptation and building regulations. In Great Britain, 74% of adults are worried about climate change.[8] They are concerned about the climate and biodiversity crisis as it impacts our daily lives, from overheating in summer to inflated energy bills in winter. They are asking us – architects, planners, engineers, developers, arboriculturists, local authorities, policy makers, industrialists – to do better.

The UK construction industry was responsible for just over 10 million tonnes of carbon dioxide in 2021 (the average house in the UK produces approximately six tonnes of carbon dioxide emissions a year). And of this, building and construction work produced nearly 1.9 million tonnes of carbon dioxide emissions.[9] In 2022, the UK residential sector alone emitted 56.4 million tonnes of carbon dioxide emissions, accounting for 17% of all carbon dioxide emissions; with the main source of emissions being natural gas for heating and cooking.[10] According to the Royal Institute of British Architects (RIBA) Business Benchmarking report released in December 2023, 60–80% of small practices' revenue comes from these residential projects, so, if we small practices act, we have the potential to bring about a huge change.

The agility of small practices to navigate these challenges cannot be understated. As small practices, we can nimbly pivot in ways medium and larger practices cannot. We can make addressing the climate crisis the primary goal of our organisations and use that to drive our proposed solutions to the housing crisis – to encourage retrofitting our existing homes rather than continuing to build new. We can make social equality – something thrown into sharp relief in the wake of the murder of George Floyd in 2020 and the subsequent Black Lives Matter demonstrations – the driving force behind our designs for equitable housing solutions. It is clear to everyone that the extractive behaviours of the Global North have had, and continue to have, dire consequences on the Global South and minority communities the world over. Without environmental sustainability we cannot have social sustainability.

A new approach will no doubt challenge us all. It will influence the projects we work on, the team members we hire, the outcomes we commit to. We will fail, iterate, fail again and iterate again. But we welcome the challenge because we believe that the evolution of small practices is key to lasting in this tumultuous state of flux our industry finds itself.

SUSTAINABLE AND REGENERATIVE DEVELOPMENT
We will address the history and impact of sustainable design and development in greater detail in subsequent chapters, but for now, we want to expand on the concepts and definitions of both 'sustainable' and 'regenerative' design and development.

While sustainable and regenerative approaches are related concepts and often overlap in certain areas, they are not the same. In their seminal book *Regenerative Development and Design: A Framework for Evolving Sustainability*, pioneers in regenerative design Pamela Mang, Ben Haggard and the Regenesis Group highlighted the move beyond the traditional approach of sustainability, emphasising not just the conservation of resources, but also the regeneration of ecosystems, communities and economies.

Conventional sustainability practices often focus on minimising harm rather than creating positive impacts. These practices, while well intentioned, are insufficient for addressing the complex environmental and societal challenges we face today. The concept of regenerative development, on the other hand, as defined by Regenesis in 1995, seeks to understand and utilise the unique characteristics of a place, creating designs that not only sustain but enhance local ecosystems, cultures and economies. Regenerative design focuses on how every place has its own potential and how design can tap into this to create thriving, resilient communities.[11]

Said another way: sustainable design focuses on *reducing the negative impact* of our built environment. It focuses us on the maxim *reduce, reuse, recycle* and has come to lean heavily (intentionally or not) on environmental challenges. Sustainability places an emphasis on *doing less harm*.

Regenerative design is about *increasing positive impact*. It focuses on the maxim *restore, renew, replenish*. Regenerative design often requires a more holistic view, considering not just a building itself but its wider impact on the ecosystem and community. It is a more ambitious approach that seeks to integrate human activities harmoniously into the natural world. Regenerative approaches place an emphasis on *doing more good*.

As practitioners looking to do things differently – to move beyond business as usual and to practise more holistically – we will need to develop our skills in understanding people and places on a much

Fig 1.4 Hermitage Mews, London, Gbolade Design Studio. This project demonstrates how small practices can work with small and medium-sized developers on small sites to deliver net-zero developments

deeper level before making decisions that alter the status quo. We must be mindful not to make short-term decisions with a linear approach, causing unintended consequences further down the line. We will need to commit to continuous learning and collaboration with our clients, our communities and our cities. We should choose to adopt place-based and potential-driven (as opposed to problem-solving) approaches to creating a thriving future.

Critically, we are now experiencing the shift in what both private and public sector clients are requesting. The priority is no longer the ordinary extension and cosmetic refurbishment or new-build home. It is more climate focused, with motivating factors ranging from increased comfort and reducing overheating to increasing carbon dioxide savings and reducing energy bills and capital costs. Many private sector clients now request more 'sustainable' or 'eco-friendly' homes. Meanwhile, government funds are available to the public sector to provide social housing decarbonisation, that is, to increase the energy efficiency of socially rented houses. We have a choice in how we respond to this ever-growing demand; a choice that must put both people and the planet first; a choice that is regenerative.

GETTING STARTED

In this book we explore our agency as architects to reclaim power and change the game. And we consider the leaders we must become if we are to change our world. We look at how other small practices have invested in research and development to create in-house carbon measuring tools. We discuss curating clients that are aligned with this vision, and how we must foster divergent thinking to maximise potential rather than just to solve problems. Here we also consider the practicalities of choosing regenerative design approaches over sustainability and look at examples of architects redefining the briefs from their clients to follow more ambitious regenerative building

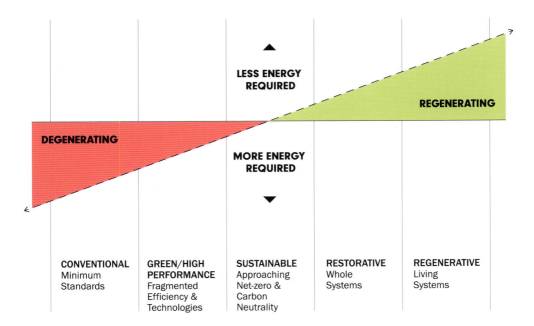

Fig 1.5 Trajectory of ecological design, source: Bill Reed, Regenesis Group

standards. We speak to practices creating their own internal standards, which they apply to all their own projects, and explore the opportunity in retrofit, acknowledging the importance of building physics. We look at embracing technological disruption and carving out new roles in a new world. We ask that we make our voices louder to influence industry change. We discover the difference between social sustainability and social value and how we might include both when adopting holistic decision-making in architecture.

Ananya Elizabeth Johnson, marine biologist, policy expert and creator of the Climate Action Venn Diagram suggests that we use our 'superpowers' for the radical changes needed to make this transition from a fossil-fuel economy to a regenerative one. Johnson's Climate Action Venn Diagram can be used as a template to identify or renew your vision. We encourage you to have a go at huddling around table and doing this collaboratively.

Large practices may have additional resources, including practice managers and sustainability teams, which we do not, but small practices have a nimbleness of spirit that cuts through the red tape and countless board director approval meetings. Aligned with a technological revolution, we believe that our size and location will no longer hold us back. We have more opportunities than ever to have a greater impact on a national and global scale; let's take advantage of it.

However, money isn't everything and the business-as-usual approach cannot be the model we adopt moving forward. Even attempts at a more 'sustainable' drive hasn't brought about the urgent change we now so desperately need. A new way of practising architecture is needed. We need a new approach that must at once embrace sustainability, as well as look beyond it. It must encompass wider socio-economic as well as environmental thinking. And it must be both sustainable and regenerative.

Fig 1.6 Climate Action Venn Diagram

YOUR PR

ACTICE

'It sounds hyperbolic, but this photograph changed my life. Or more accurately it changed my mind. Our first years growing Just Eat went well but we soon outgrew our student customer niche. We found ourselves competing nationally with two insurmountable competitors: the telephone and Dominos.

Around this time, we were introduced to Adam Morgan, author of Eating the Big Fish, who showed this sweet photo of a little boy facing off with a giant sumo. Adam asked a simple question – who would win this fight? Obviously, the sumo. Then Adam asked, who would win this race? Very different outcome.

Reframing the competition this way is how small insurgent teams can tackle seemingly insurmountable habits and behaviours in the market. At Just Eat, we stopped focusing on explaining online food delivery and became entertainers, developing advertising and content that was part of a great night in. Within a few years we had outperformed both our terrifying competitors and had become the number one method of ordering takeaway in the UK.'[1]
— Mat Braddy, former Chief Marketing Officer of Just Eat

THE POWER OF SMALL

The Just Eat story is an inspirational one; it is a lesson in exploring alternative perspectives and taking a more unexpected route to success. It is important, though, to think critically about what 'success' means for you and your practice.

This chapter explores creating, refining and running a future-proofed small practice through a regenerative, value-driven, decision-making lens. As highlighted in the previous chapter, a regenerative approach moves beyond the old sustainable mantra of reduce, reuse, recycle towards one of restore, renew, replenish. In adopting a regenerative lens in practice, we aim to explore the mindset we will need as small practices to break through and disrupt a market dominated by larger, established players. Here too we look at small practices that have a clear and strong sense of who they are and what they stand for.

Our traditional role as providers of a physical service is necessarily shifting to one in which we are also called upon by clients to understand, translate and curate important information about sustainability and regenerative thinking. Now we are not only required to help clients identify if we are meeting certain targets, but also to help define which targets are necessary to meet, and how we will continue to adapt to new targets in the future. To do this well we need a new type of leadership: leadership that is generous; leadership that is transparent.

THE REGENERATIVE LEADER

A regenerative practice requires a new type of leader: one who can address our deeply wounded world and bring it to a new place of healing. We are working with a new generation; a generation that, despite being overwhelmed by climate anxiety, is steaming ahead to create a world that is environmentally responsible. At the same time, they are fighting for social equality and engaging in hard conversations about equity and diversity. It is clear that they are moulding themselves into the types of leaders they have searched for, but not yet found.

An example of such a leader is Mikaela Loach, a Jamaican-born climate activist who lives in the UK. Loach believes that tackling the climate crisis will require us to revisit the roots of capitalist exploitation to enable us to dismantle the foundations of the issues we face in society today. In her book *It's Not That Radical: Climate Action to Transform Our World*, Loach emphasises that true

CHAPTER 2   YOUR PRACTICE   **21**

Fig 2.1 The sumo wrestler versus the boy. Redefining the rules of the game

Fig 2.2 Mikaela Loach, climate activist and author of *It's Not That Radical: Climate Action to Transform Our World*

climate action requires a systemic change, addressing the roots of issues such as poverty, capitalist exploitation, police brutality and legal injustice, arguing that the climate crisis cannot be separated from these social injustices and that climate justice is integral to achieving racial equality and collective liberation. She maintains that we should measure all these contributors (rather than the narrow view of environmental sustainability) as a key success determinant.[2] Indeed, the regenerative leader measures social and environmental impact as success parameters, alongside profitability. As Alan Moore, business transformation coach and author, observes, we should regard society as our main stakeholder, not merely as a shareholder. Furthermore, we are to 'consider leadership for a progressive business as being inspirational, creative, empathetic, compassionate and inclusive. This is a leadership that is rooted not in power and authority; its strength lies in transformative service and wisdom'.[3]

In our experience, many small practice leaders have many of these qualities in spades already. But to become a transformational and regenerative leader we must take a longer view. A generational view, rather than one-year, five-year or even ten-year business plan. We are to make decisions adopting a generational lens. In a world where 'efficiency' and 'productivity' loom large, can a regenerative perspective make space for a so-called longer now? The regenerative leader must be able to bring their personal hopes, dreams, aspirations and authenticity into the professional realm, and if necessary, be willing to change these.

	EXTRACTION ECONOMY	**REGENERATIVE ECONOMY**
Value creation metrics	Takings	Contributions
Main stakeholder	Shareholder interest	Societal interest
Success parameter	Financial valuation	Social impact
Growth paradigm	Exponential	Circular
Perspective/Life cycle	Short term	Long term
Workforce	Human resource	Resourceful humans
Divisions of labour	Departments	Communities
Leadership	Command and control	Inspire and motivate
Organisation	Structure	Culture

Table 2.1 Value creation metrics of a regenerative economy, source: Alan Moore and Mads Thimmer

CHAPTER 2 YOUR PRACTICE

CASE STUDY

PRACTICE PROFILE:
NIMTIM ARCHITECTS

Fig 2.3 nimtim co-founders Tim O'Callaghan and Nimi Attanayake (far left) with their team

REGENERATIVE LEADERSHIP: PRACTICING RADICAL TRANSPARENCY

Implementing a regenerative vision needs radical transparency from leadership and the team. nimtim architects demonstrate this by sharing all salary details with the whole office such that all team members know what other team members are paid. All staff members are empowered to recognise that they all have project and process targets to meet, which of course impact project cost and the profitability of the business. The practice also recently catalogued, and publicly shared, the experience of searching for a new junior member of staff. As a result of this process, they called upon the industry to rethink their approach to valuing architects' services.

In 2023, nimtim advertised for a new Part 1 position and listed the salary as 'upwards of £26,000', which they thought was a decent wage for the level of experience required (and in accordance with the industry going rate). However, feedback revealed that while the salary was in line with the London Living Wage, it still wasn't considered enough to live on in London. After undertaking some investigations, including researching average rent prices, bills and commuting costs, they conceded that £26,000 did not leave very much spare change. In fact, the salary was equal to, or less than, working at a London pub or coffee shop. This seemed unfair, particularly when considering the training required, the level of responsibility and the liability taken on by the architect.

As a result, nimtim decided to increase the salary. Founding director of nimtim, Tim O'Callaghan, highlighted this in his piece in the *Architects Journal* stating: 'I believe low pay is the biggest contributor to the profession's woeful lack of representation. It creates an exclusionary working environment that puts up barriers that prevent people from lower income backgrounds and under-represented groups from entering the profession.'[4]

nimtim's desire to be a good employer, and the their willingness to discuss the issue publicly,

Fig 2.4 Early ideas for corner plots in Becontree, nimtim

demonstrates a wider awareness of issues within the profession. They opened up the conversation, addressing not just economic challenges but also those related to access, and they looked to address the social ecosystem that retains the status quo.

This radical transparency sparked a wider conversation in the industry regarding awareness around poor employment practices and low pay in the profession, particularly in the context of the 'successful' perception of architecture as a career path. In addition, conversations around how architects value their work began. These addressed the paradox of the low fees charged against an ever-increasing level of complexity and expertise required (take the new Building Safety Act, or the new principal designer role, or the technical, sustainable and regenerative design standards, for example).

The solution, nimtim felt, came from grassroots campaign groups within the industry, such as the Future Architects Front (FAF) and the Section of Architectural Workers (SAW) union, which have raised awareness of poor employment practices. nimtim highlight that this is a problem the industry ultimately needs to solve collectively, bringing a spirit of solidarity that many younger colleagues are already demonstrating, while stopping the proverbial race to the bottom.

Now, how do you think the newly employed staff member will feel being paid a decent wage? More than likely valued. And how do you think they might show up to the office if they feel valued? Perhaps empowered to be fully involved and fully authentic in their work. We believe that this type of radical transparency is regenerative because nimtim challenged the industry to renew its views on business-as-usual when it comes employment. They moved beyond the isolated issue and tapped into the wider economic and social fabric of a problem that could eventually leave the industry in a far worse state. Their example demonstrates that strength lies in transformative service and wisdom over size.

DEVELOPING A REGENERATIVE VISION

Having a team who feel valued and empowered cannot be left to chance; it has to form part of a concerted effort to change the status quo. It must be part of a practice's vision of their regenerative future. Developing a regenerative vision into a company requires a strategic approach that aligns with core business functions and involves stakeholders at all levels. That is, bringing the team along and empowering them to have agency within the business.

Setting targets

Over 40% of small practices have taken the bold step of signing the UK Architects Declare Climate and Biodiversity Emergency declaration.[5] This advocates for faster change in regard to the climate crisis and the adoption of more regenerative design principles with the aim of going beyond net zero, supporting those working for climate justice and striving to ensure equity and an improved quality of life for all. We are choosing to meet and exceed the Low Energy Transformation Initiative (LETI) and RIBA 2023 Climate Challenge targets over the government's Building Regulations. Practices are also committing to the UK Green Building Council's (UKGBC) Net Zero Carbon Buildings Framework that sets out high-level principles for achieving net-zero carbon for construction and for operational energy.[6] In some cases, they are aligning with local authority sustainability guidance and targets, which move beyond policy and have material planning weight such as the Harlow & Gilston Garden Town Sustainability Guidance and Checklist.[7]

Our industry is rapidly getting to grips with the influx of new standards and targets, including revised versions of the Royal Institution of Chartered Surveyors' (RICS) Whole Life Carbon Analysis (WLCA) and the UK Net Zero Carbon Building Standard (2024). We expect that many more will also start choosing to align with regenerative metrics akin to the International Living Future Institute's (ILFI) Living Building Challenge (LBC) targets (we expand on this in the next chapter).

In any event, your practice will likely need its own internal goals, decision-making frameworks, objectives and key results. But committing to industry standards is a good place to start.

Measuring what matters

We believe that business can do good. To do so, the regenerative leader must measure success both quantitatively and qualitatively. Performance measures must focus on social, environmental and economic parameters in order to build a progressive business that prioritises people and the planet. As you transform your company into a regenerative-led business, having objectives and key results that everyone in the practice can align with and commit to becomes imperative.

According to business guru John Doerr, objectives and key results (OKRs) are collaborative goal-setting processes that ensures a business focuses effort on the same important issues. The objective is *what* should be achieved, and the key results benchmark and monitor how to reach the objective.

In running a small practice ourselves, we have found that using a grounded decision-making framework through OKRs and practice-wide questions has been useful in helping us make the best decisions for the business. This decision-making process stops us from falling into the trap of taking on a project for the sake of cashflow alone – leading to unfulfilled work, tense relationships with clients or misaligned project outcomes.

Decision-making framework

As small practice leaders trying to navigate this rapidly changing world, we are always stretched for time. We straddle working *in* the business and working *on* the business, alongside project delivery and business stability. We split our focus between business development and existing client satisfaction, and are constantly exploring new sectors while trying to remain innovative in existing ones. All of that without even a mention of our family or personal lives.

OKRs are therefore critical for the proper execution of great (and regenerative) ideas. They are fun to create and involve business owners and employees. While a practice owner might set the overall objective (often qualitative), the key results (usually quantitative) can be created together by the team so everyone has the opportunity to be committed from the outset. So, what do regenerative OKRs look like? That is, objectives and key results that restore, renew and replenish? OKRs are helpful precisely because of their simplicity; because they allow us to focus, commit to our goals, align with our small team and track for accountability.

The table below details regenerative business OKRs for the first quarter of a year. They are designed to renew our ambition of playing our part in addressing the climate emergency. While it might seem small in the larger context, we are convinced that, if all small practices play their part, we might just move the dial to a more equitable world.

OBJECTIVE 1		Gain two new domestic projects with a construction budget of >£200,000
KEY RESULTS	1	Develop and implement four-week social media strategy that posts weekly on retrofit projects we have delivered and prioritises communicating our technical expertise on this subject.
	2	Prioritise projects that include a good percentage of the £200,000 construction budget to be focused on fabric upgrade to LETI best practice targets.
	3	One staff member/director to enrol in Retrofit Academy PAS2035 Retrofit Course to commence in Q2 of this year.
OBJECTIVE 2		Sustainable work/life balance for all team members (including director(s))
KEY RESULTS	1	Prioritise quarterly team check-ins to understand their views on workload and stress, then collectively devise plan to address both.
	2	Consider hybrid working/4-day week as a team and discuss the benefits and challenges to the business and work/life balance of all team members.
	3	Interview staff candidates with a view to offering a part-time position to start in Q2/Q3 of this year; based on cashflow and helping relieve staff overworking.
	4	Create project case study templates for three projects to reduce the amount of upfront collective work required to bid for new projects, driving team efficiency and reducing team workload.

Table 2.2 Example of regenerative business OKRs

CASE STUDY

PRACTICE PROFILE: KNOX BHAVAN ARCHITECTS

DEVELOPING A REGENERATIVE VISION:
PRIORITISING RESEARCH AND DEVELOPMENT

An example of a small practice who argue for collaboration in defining goals, and who have played their part in addressing our climate emergency, is London-based Knox Bhavan Architects. A key OKR for this practice is research and development.

Sustainable solutions provide an excellent opportunity to expand in-house research and development. This inspired Knox Bevan to create the KBe tool an in-house carbon calculator that examines, communicates and reduces the embodied carbon of projects they work on. It emphasises the potential in sustainable solutions, benefitting both their firm and providing a unique offering to their clients.

The development of the KBe tool was led by Ben Hair, who leads on sustainability within the practice. The process began by auditing the practice's built projects and finding that, while things could be improved, there was inherent knowledge within the practice about designing low-carbon buildings through material choice and efficient and elegant structures.

OBJECTIVE 1		Encourage team to explore interests that develop the knowledge and growth of the business
KEY RESULTS	1	Sustainability lead in practice to develop an in-house tool using readily accessible data from existing Knox Bhavan projects.
	2	Project research and development to last maximum of one year, and less if possible.
	3	Develop wider company learning and adoption of the tool to be rolled out across practice.

Table 2.3 Example of a regenerative practice OKRs

The next step involved overcoming the challenges of carbon literacy within the practice – that is, the need to develop an awareness and understanding of the carbon costs and impacts of everyday activities, as well as the ability and motivation to reduce emissions on an individual, community and company level so as to make better informed decisions – within the practice, developing the tool meant adopting a three-pronged approach including measuring material quantities and carbon factors to establish the embodied carbon of a design; using 3D building information modelling (BIM); and drawing on external carbon data sources such as LETI and the inventory of carbon and energy (ICE) database. The next stage was about communication. The KBe tool uses a dial to visualise embodied carbon in orange segments, sequestered carbon in green and the retention or demolition of existing structure embodied carbon in yellow. The final stage was to reduce carbon. Once an understanding of the embodied carbon distribution is clear – perhaps, for example, the floor construction is performing badly – this knowledge can be used to look at alternative options for design or material substitution.

This process not only demonstrates Knox Bhavan's willingness to embrace a changing market, but also shows the readiness and ability of leadership to encourage team members to explore research that ends up benefitting the company.

A key point here is the acknowledgment that this tool, like many others out there, will need continual development and might never be finished. This is important because many find that the overwhelming nature of sustainable and regenerative design acts as a barrier. The KBe tool is informed by the projects the practice has worked on and, as a result, also informs the future work of the practice, creating a perpetual iterative process that will lead to refinement as the practice continues to develop the tool.

Practices like Knox Bhavan Architects, who see themselves evolving to meet the needs of society at large and committing to research and development, we believe, demonstrate regenerative thinking and decision-making.

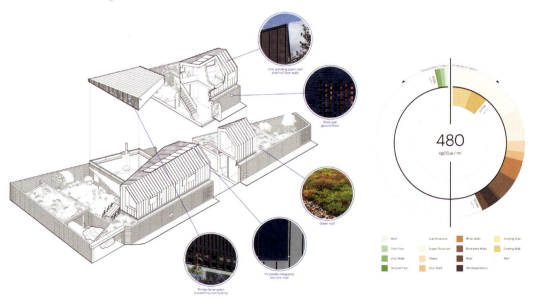

Fig 2.5 KBe, Knox Bhavan's carbon calculator tool

Here are some questions that could be asked of your practice team before embarking on a project as a way of outlining and defining your OKRs moving forward.

Alignment with core values and vision: Does this project align with our business's core values, mission and vision? Will it further our goals and enhance our reputation in the direction we want? Will we learn something new? Will undertaking this project challenge our usual way of doing things? Can we incorporate any lessons into new projects?

Client relationship: Is the client's vision, expectation and communication style compatible with ours? Have we vetted the client's track record, reliability and reputation in the industry?

Feasibility and capability: Do we have the expertise, resources and capacity to execute this project successfully? Are the project's timelines, budget and scope realistic and manageable for our team? What impact could taking on this project have on our team (learning opportunity, quality, health and well-being)?

Economic viability: Is the project financially viable for our firm? Will it generate an adequate return on investment, considering both immediate and long-term benefits? Are there hidden costs or potential financial risks associated with the project?

Potential impact and legacy: What will be the social, environmental and cultural impact of this project (to the team, to the end users and to the planet)? Does it present opportunities for innovation, learning and growth for our team? Will this project leave a positive legacy that we can be proud of?

These questions can help architecture businesses evaluate potential projects holistically, ensuring that they take on work that is not only profitable but also meaningful and aligned with their broader goals and principles.

CURATING YOUR CLIENTS

If we are transforming our leadership and our practices to become regenerative, then the lifeline of our businesses – that is, our clients – must be involved. After all, they are the ones who typically ensure that we start and stay in business. We might choose, to a degree, the projects we want to work on, but who we work with and for is just as important. Our clients must align with our values.

Thankfully, a new generation is emerging across all client types. We've certainly observed that our clients' needs have changed. From one-off domestic clients to boutique developers, and from large PLCs to local authorities, all clients need to play their part in responding to our climate emergency and prioritising quality living for all people.

We have also observed that their reasons for change are just as varied as the client types themselves: from PLCs needing to report to shareholders and to meet environmental, social and governance (ESG) targets, to planning departments responding to cabinet members and portfolio holders who have asked the local authority to declare a climate emergency and from private sector developers working to reduce the risk of planning application refusal to homeowners wishing to explore new renewable energy technology and reduced energy bills. Even financial backers are getting in on the action, with banks like Lloyds offering favourable interest rates for sustainable developments through their sustainability-backed funding schemes and sustainability finance frameworks. Private funders, such as Atelier Finance, are offering bespoke loan solutions to back net-zero developments. From the carrot to the stick, whatever the reason, this change is a good change.

As businesses, success will increasingly be defined by our values. As small practices, we need to ensure our leadership direction and business goals are translated to our clients. Through such changes in client type and client motivation, we can now have more choices for the type of client we want to align ourselves with – more choice than we've ever had. While it might be challenging for larger practices to shift and change their client base, our nimble nature as small practices really comes to the fore. Here, we can shine. Here, we can lead the way.

The goal isn't just to attract any client, but to attract those who resonate with, and value, the principles of sustainable and regenerative design. By positioning itself as an expert in this still growing niche and actively engaging with a target audience, a small practice can effectively curate a client base that has a shared vision. Curating a client base involves a combination of demonstrating expertise, leveraging appropriate marketing and outreach strategies and cultivating relationships with people that align with these vision and values.

Building a regenerative client list will involve either working with some existing clients to bring them on the journey, or it might mean choosing to not work with them going forward. This might seem

Fig 2.6 A sustainability-minded project client of Gbolade Design Studio, where pupils from a local girls school were invited on-site during the build to learn about net-zero construction

brutal, but is this not necessary if we are to move beyond business as usual? Mike Michalowicz, author of *The Pumpkin Plan,* devised a client assessment chart – a strategic tool designed to help service-based small businesses identify which clients are most beneficial to their growth and success.[8] Michalowicz's assessment chart focuses on an evaluation criterion including revenue amount, payment speed, communication quality and repeat work, to help small businesses identify the clients they want to keep working with. This assessment chart is incredibly useful and has helped thousands of small businesses worldwide (including ours) to see, in the cold light of day, which clients might be working best for them, and which should be let go. However, we wondered, if we took Michalowicz's chart and refined it to include regenerative business evaluation criterion of our own, what would this look like? The basic premise of the client assessment chart involves writing a list of all current clients, then ordering them in the context of which clients provide the largest revenue over a planned period (say a year), which ones are great communicators when things go awry, which offer repeat work and which make your face light up when their call comes through on your phone.

See below an example of a worked client evaluation chart:

THE CLIENT ASSESSMENT CHART

Client name	Client revenue over 12 months	Enjoyability: are they joyful to work with?	Do they settle invoices quickly?	Opportunity for repeat revenue/ referral	Do they communicate well?	Are they aligned with our sustainability/ regenerative goals?	Total
Client 1	£73,000	3	6	9	8	5	31
Client 2	£58,800	7	9	8	9	10	43
Client 3	£48,000	9	10	8	3	8	38
Client 4	£42,200	5	5	8	8	3	29
Client 5	£23,800	4	7	2	4	6	23

Table 2.4 Client evaluation chart, adapted from *The Pumpkin Plan* by Mike Michalowicz. A practice might reasonably decide that the highest score equates to their favourite client.
(Note: this might not be the client who brings in the greatest revenue).

In creating an expanded assessment criterion, we can ask questions such as: what is a client's sustainability/regenerative value? What do clients *profess* they want versus what do they *actually* do? How likely are they to be influenced by our own business's regenerative practices? Will working with this client enliven or depress our team?

This exercise is important for small practices because with our limited time and resources, who we spend our time with matters. It matters because if we are to deliver our best service, then it must be to the best clients. The ones who are coming along this transformative journey with us. The ones that, despite not having it all figured out, are willing to be educated with us along the way. Therefore, identifying who those key partners are matters. The saying 'yes' to everyone strategy cannot be sustained.

Guidelines for applying the principles
Define a shared niche: Understand the specifics of your regenerative approach and if your existing/new clients align with this. What is unique about how this client might implement regenerative practices – do they focus on:

– the urban regeneration scale
– sustainable materials
– ecosystem restoration
– or a combination?

This will require concerted effort in learning what you want out of your client, so researching the type of client you want is key.

Build a strong portfolio: Showcase projects that emphasise your regenerative principles – this need not be completed projects, but instead those that demonstrate the thinking behind a regenerative approach. It is also worth noting that aspects of a project can count towards a strong portfolio. For example, if a scheme was only able to embed green roofs in a project, or if it was able to retain trees that were initially planned for removal, these are all wins that demonstrate a movement towards the overall goal.

Educate potential clients: Offer workshops, seminars or webinars on the benefits and principles of regenerative design. This will not only educate potential clients but also position you as an authority in the field. Examples include feeding-in to a client's already planned continuing professional development (CPD) programme so you are seamlessly working within a framework they already have, rather than trying to chart a new course within their ever-busy calendars.

Engage with industry: Attend conferences, workshops and seminars related to sustainable and regenerative design. Network with like-minded professionals and potential clients. Look for opportunities to contribute to panels (rather than full-blown speaking), as a good way to demonstrate expertise to your ideal clients.

Collaborate: This is a theme that will come up again and again. Work with other professionals, such as permaculturists, sustainable landscape architects or green technology providers, to offer comprehensive solutions.

Reach out directly: Identify potential clients who are already leaning towards sustainable or eco-friendly projects. This might include businesses with a strong corporate social responsibility mandate, non-profits working in environmental sectors or developers keen on green building. Identify if you are offering a business-to-business and/or business-to-customer service and develop the relevant strategies to reach either or both.

Host site visits: If possible, arrange for potential clients to visit completed projects to see the regenerative principles in action. Curate the guestlist to include existing clients where repeat work can be harnessed, or potential clients where you can demonstrate completion of works – this is particularly of importance to new or pivoting practices.

Seek testimonials: Clients who've had a positive experience working with you can be your best promoters. Encourage them to share their experiences and outcomes. For clients who have not had the best experience with your practice for a host of reasons (staff shortage, project mismanagement, your energy), try to salvage the relationship and ask how you can improve. At the very least, this allows you to learn from and refine your processes.

Develop a strong online presence: Maintain a website that clearly articulates your philosophy, services and past projects. Regularly publish blog posts or articles on topics related to regenerative design. This gives you an opportunity to launch, then relaunch, then relaunch again – keeping your practice front and centre of a client's mind. Just think, every time Beyoncé sells-out a new world tour, this is her relaunch, again and again and again. Generating new fans, embedding loyal fans and staying profitable so she can continue to do what she loves – create.

Collaborate with educational institutions: Offer to give guest lectures or run workshops at architectural schools or related programme, thereby influencing and connecting with the next generation of clients and collaborators.

FOSTERING DIVERGENT THINKING

To address and bring restorative practices to the world's most complex problems we will need innovative ways of thinking, and for this we need everyone at the table. This includes those who have historically been left out of the decision-making room – to the detriment of society and our planet. A regenerative business should seek to include those whose voices have been marginalised and silenced for far too long, and those who no longer aspire to enter such rooms and have become resigned to the status quo.

While we are desperate to move on from the debate about diversity in the workplace, alas, here we still find ourselves. You may not be surprised to read that in the UK there are more women out of employment than there are men in employment. Or that of those in work, most are born in the UK. Taking London as an example, 37% of Londoners are immigrants (that is, they were born in a different country).[9] In the 2020/21 records, the largest share came from India, followed by Nigeria, Poland, Italy, Romania, Portugal, Spain, United States, Australia, Germany and Ireland. What is interesting is that most men in work who come from immigrant backgrounds come from the United States, Australia, Germany and Ireland.[10] It is clear that a Western education system is valued here in the UK. This would be fine if we didn't know that homogenous thinking is adversely impacting the rate of innovation in the UK. Evidence shows that despite our robust research infrastructure, the UK lags behind its global competitors in adopting and implementing new ideas and technologies, ranking eleventh in knowledge diffusion and twenty-seventh in knowledge absorption.[11]

The adoption of innovation plays a crucial role in our economic growth; 44% of the GDP per capita variance among countries is attributed to technology diffusion. Enhancing the uptake of innovative concepts and technologies in UK firms, along with their commercialisation, is pivotal for boosting productivity, job creation and economic recovery. The UK's prominent position in international research collaboration, a key factor in achieving a higher scientific impact, reinforces its status as a preferred partner in global innovation. For sustained innovation, however, the UK must support these collaborative efforts. Furthermore, businesses are increasingly recognising a shortage of qualified personnel as a barrier to innovation. If it doesn't address this shortage as a matter of urgency, the UK faces imminent skills gaps in digital, management and science, technology, engineering and maths (STEM) areas. It's crucial for our workforce, as well as for our educational and training systems, to be sufficiently diverse, broad and scalable to meet the demands of a more innovative economy and society.[12]

In their 2019 study 'The Heterogenous Impact of Market Size on Innovation: Evidence from French Firm Level Exports', Aghion and colleagues showed that diversifying the export markets for a country's products and services can lead to immediate increases in sales and employment.[13]

This boost in economic activity encourages other firms to enter the export market, which creates a competitive environment. As a result, more productive local firms are spurred to enhance their innovation activities in order to maintain their competitive advantage. This dynamic illustrates the interplay between market diversification, competition and innovation within an economy. The study underscores the importance of export market diversification as a catalyst for economic growth and innovation. By expanding into new markets, firms not only increase their own growth potential but also contribute to a more competitive and innovative local business environment. This can have a far-reaching impact on the overall economy, fostering a cycle of growth, competition and innovation.

In his book *Rebel Ideas: The Power of Diverse Thinking*, Matthew Syed introduces the concept of 'recombinant ideas', which refers to the innovation that occurs when ideas from different cultures (and fields) are combined.[14] This type of innovation is contrasted with incremental innovation, which involves small improvements within a specific field. Recombinant ideas are significant because they allow for a broader and more creative perspective, bringing together diverse opinions and disciplines. This process enables ideas and topics to be viewed from an external standpoint and provides clearer insights compared with being deeply immersed in the intricacies of a single field. The connective and multiplying effect of new ideas inspires further innovation and enhances productivity. An example we're all too familiar with is the tool we have in our hands most of the time, the mobile phone – but more specifically, the iPhone. For better or for worse, this innovation represents a fusion of ideas about telephones and computers, combining these distinct fields to create a revolutionary product that has changed how we operate forever.

In the 21st century, the most exciting, innovative and life-changing ideas that could change the planet and humankind for good will be recombinant ideas. If we are to look to find the best and most inclusive solutions to our climate and biodiversity emergencies, addressing how we adopt recombinant ideas to spark innovation is key.

In their 2018 'Delivering through Diversity', management consultants McKinsey & Company highlighted that having women in senior positions and maintaining ethnically diverse organisations can lead to a whopping 66% increase in profitability.[15] They highlighted the clear link between diversity (a greater proportion of women and a more mixed ethnic and cultural composition in leadership) and financial outperformance of companies. Their analysis draws on data from over 1,000 companies across 12 countries including the UK, United States, South Africa, Brazil, Mexico and Singapore.

Key findings included:

Gender diversity: Companies in the top quartile for gender diversity on their leadership teams were found to be 21% more likely to have above average profitability compared with those in the bottom quartile. This is because gender diverse leadership teams brought a wider range of perspectives and experiences to the table, approaching problems and opportunities from multiple angles. They had an improved understanding of the customer base, particularly in the consumer markets, and they had enhanced talent attraction and retention, making them more competitive. This correlation between gender diversity and profitability was consistent across geographies, highlighting the role of executive teams in strategic and operational decision making and its impact on financial performance.

Ethnic and cultural diversity: Companies with the most ethnically diverse executive teams were 33% more likely to outperform their peers on profitability. This is because, again, a broader range of perspectives were brought to bear, including different cultural backgrounds leading to varied ways of thinking, problem solving and decision making. This diversity in thought and approach fosters creativity and innovation, leading to more effective business strategies and solutions. In addition, in an increasingly globalised business environment, having leaders with diverse ethnic backgrounds provides valuable insights into different markets. This can be particularly advantageous for businesses looking to expand or operate internationally, as it aids in understanding various customer preferences, cultural nuances and market dynamics. McKinsey found that diverse teams are often more innovative and effective in problem solving, with the ability to quickly adapt to changes in the market and to be more resilient in the face of challenges.

More broadly, the report assumes that more diverse companies are better able to attract top talent, improve customer orientation and employee satisfaction, and enhance decision making. These factors contribute to a company's overall performance and ability to maintain its license to operate. Despite the challenges of improving diversity and inclusion, companies that have made significant efforts in these areas have seen tangible benefits.

McKinsey's report highlights the importance of diversity in leadership roles, not only as a matter of social justice or corporate responsibility but as a strategic business advantage leading to higher profitability and value creation.

Even if women and people of colour enter leadership positions, they must face the gauntlet of 1,000 cuts along the way. This was reported by finding Sonal Kumar, Assistant Professor of Finance at Bryant University, in her recently published study 'When distinction disguises discrimination: A look at female and non-white CEO performance' – a paper chosen as the best paper in the diversity, equity and inclusion (DEI) category by the Academy of Management Annual Conference in

Fig 2.7 Black Females in Architecture (BFA)

Boston and published in the Academy of Management 2023 proceedings.[16] Having focused on top performing companies in the United States, the results of the study suggest that among the groups experiencing heightened discrimination (women and people of colour (POC)), those individuals who endured the most challenges emerged as the top performers. They found that higher levels of discrimination faced by certain groups correlated with superior performance among the most resilient members of these groups. The underlying reason for these findings is that increased discrimination and scrutiny require individuals to be more capable to reach the position of CEO. In essence, the study suggests that the female and minoritised CEOs, especially those who are top performers, have had to demonstrate extraordinary capability to overcome the additional barriers they face.

In the UK, women represent 28% of architects, which is significantly lower than in professions such as accountancy (44%), medicine (45%) and law (47%), and surprising considering that women make up a near even split when starting university (51.5%).[17] When looking at leadership positions specifically, in the largest 100 practices in the UK, women make up 21% of leadership positions and in small practices the share of women in leadership positions is lower still, at 15–18%![18]

Eleven percent of architects are from Black, Asian or Minority Ethnic groups in the UK. In our industry, just 1% of architects (men and women) are Black or Black British, according to the Architects Registration Board (ARB), which gathers data from the 43,000 architects registered with the professional body.[19] We have no numbers for minoritised groups in leadership positions, but given the woeful numbers for women in leadership positions, it's fair to assume that this figure is scarily lower. This dearth of information indicates a need for more comprehensive and accessible data on diversity and inclusion within the architecture industry, particularly concerning the representation of ethnically diverse individuals in various roles and the impact of diversity on firm performance and employee well-being.

Anecdotally, the Paradigm Network (a professional network in the UK that champions Black and Asian representation in the built environment, with over 700 members) raised this topic in 2020 at the height of the Black Lives Matter protests following the murder of George Floyd. The goal was simple: to see how many in a discussion group aspired to leadership positions within their practices. The response was depressing, less than 5% of the 30 people present aspired to leadership positions. Barriers to aspiration ranged from not wanting to commit to a practice that did not appreciate their value through to the resignation that they had never seen anyone who looked like them in those positions and therefore did not expect to witness any tangible change from the business owners.

Social enterprises like Black Females in Architecture (BFA) continue to strive to change the status quo. The intersectional nature of the Black female experience informs how they occupy and hope to design our everyday spaces. In an increasingly globalised society, BFA seeks to challenge a solely Western understanding of the built environment towards a more equitable approach to city-making.

It's easy to become despondent given the figures above reflecting the representation of women and minoritised groups, yet we see this new, regenerative practice as one that faces these challenges head-on and makes changes for the greater good.

Imagine this: a society where the people most marginalised are brought into the room and sat down around the decision-making table. What ideas are we currently missing out on because we are so used to the status quo? What great innovations have we overlooked because we glorify a Western way of thinking, doing, being? What regenerative solutions have our climate and species foregone because we've gotten in our own way?

These issues, while complex, overlap with daily life, and many of your team are living through the constant trauma of reopening closed wounds – even as they attempt to lend their voice and fund aid to condemn wars. This 'distraction' weighs heavy on the hearts of your teams, who may not feel they have a safe space for complex discussions. Could we allow our working environments to enable those conversations? Imagine what might happen in your business when your Part 2 employee comes to the table authentically? Imagine what jewels may lie behind a true answer to the question 'how are you coping while your country of birth is at war?'

Yet, if we are transforming our practices into regenerative places – places that renew and restore society, places that have people and planet as our stakeholder – we must ask ourselves, can we really afford to leave some of our best players off the field?

Guidelines for applying the principles

To embark on the journey of becoming a regenerative leader and practice – one that fights for a more equitable society and planet – it is crucial to engage in both formal and informal learning experiences with other leaders.

The UKGBC plays a pivotal role in this context. It offers a learning and leadership portfolio that includes short, accessible courses and immersive learning experiences in live projects. Its programmes aim to increase awareness, deepen sustainability knowledge and enhance skills across

Fig 2.8 UKGBC Future Leaders programme, Summer 2023 cohort

four levels: raising awareness, building understanding, developing expertise and driving change. Its goal is to empower individuals to contribute to a net-zero, climate-resilient and regenerative built environment. The UKGBC's Future Leaders programme is particularly noteworthy. It brings together high-potential professionals from various sectors for a unique leadership and innovation programme. This initiative aims to inspire the next generation of leaders to transform the sustainability of the built environment.

Another significant programme is offered by Regenesis Group, the Regenerative Practitioner series. This five-month course delves deeply into the shifts in thinking and practice needed for regenerative development. The course, developed over 25 years, introduces regenerative concepts and frameworks. Participants, organised in geographically based cohorts, engage closely with peers and instructors. The programme is not merely training but a profound exploration of new perspectives on work. It involves significant internal transformation in the participants' thinking and working methods. The course consists of 10 two-hour dialogue sessions via Zoom, supplemented with reading materials and exercises, culminating in a three-day intensive workshop, often held in person.

ENVIRON
REGENER

MENTAL
ATION

Ella Adoo-Kissi-Debrah was a nine-year-old, medal-winning gymnast. She enjoyed sports and music and had a particular love for the cornet. She dreamed of becoming a pilot and was the centre of her family's world.

Ella lived in Lewisham, south-east London, just near the South Circular road, and walked to school every day along this road. The last two to three years of her life were punctuated by severe asthma attacks and in February 2013 Ella tragically died. Following investigations it was found that Ella's route to school had some of the highest air pollution rates in London, generated by nearby traffic and exceeding the EU legal limit. Ella was the first person in the UK to have air pollution listed as a cause of death on her death certificate.

Her mother, Rosamund, campaigned and advocated consistently in the seven years following Ella's death; and following an inquest and a landmark ruling in December 2021, 'Ella's Law' saw the UK declare the right to clean air as a human right.

Ella is one of 33,000 people in the UK who die annually from poor air quality. Rosamund has played a critical role in ensuring that this type of death does not affect more people, including children. Rosamund said during the inquest that if she had known the risks air pollution posed to Ella she would have moved house.

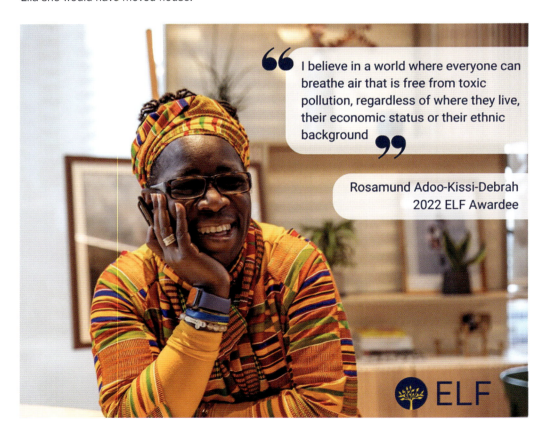

Fig 3.1 Rosamund Adoo-Kissi-Debrah, founder, director and trustee of the Ella Roberta Foundation

THE POWER OF SMALL

Rosamund Adoo-Kissi-Debrah's story is one of climate justice, of advocacy and of long-term resilience. It has the power to inspire us, as small-practice architects, to recognise our power in making sustained, long-term, effective changes. The daily decisions we make as architects matter in a way that might mean life or death to everyday people: from how we choose to orientate housing and locate habitable rooms to the quality of indoor air and comfort; and from designing-out fuel poverty to providing appropriate pedestrian and cycling routes for communities. Thinking and designing beyond the red line is a necessity architects and urban designers (no matter the size of their practices) must embrace more holistically – being intentional about understanding the environmental, societal and economic impacts of our decision making.

As a society, we are now wrapping our heads around the impact of climate change, and we as architects are starting to get to grips with the measures we must now deploy. This chapter argues for why sustainability is no longer an option for us; for how we must go beyond sustaining (doing no further harm) and race towards a more regenerative way of being in order to halt the damage we have already done to our planet, preserve the good that exists and enhance these ecosystems so that people and planet can thrive into the future.

A PARADIGM SHIFT: BEYOND SUSTAINABLE, TOWARDS REGENERATIVE

S&P Global Commodity Insights reported that in 2022 investments in renewable power and energy storage reached approximately $477 billion, with this figure projected to average $700 billion annually through 2030 and an anticipation that between 2023 and 2050, renewable power will comprise 70–75% of all new installed generating capacity.[1] In 2023, the BBC's *Panorama* programme aired an episode addressing the government's ambition to ban sales of new gas boilers from 2035 and its goal to roll out 600,000 new heat pump installations each year by 2028 – albeit with a significant gap in meeting this target.[2] It is evident that the message is being received as we are now voting with our funds. Yet progress also seems slow.

In the summer of 2022, leading organisations including the RIBA, UKGBC and RICS joined forces to launch the UK's first cross-industry Net Zero Carbon (NZC) Building Standard – addressing all major building types. Amidst an industry riddled with varying targets, which often contribute to the feeling of being overwhelmed and in some cases lead to inaction, the UK NZC Building Standard hopes to establish a clear, unified definition and methodology for achieving net zero in the UK building sector. This standard will allow the industry to effectively demonstrate that their built assets achieve net-zero carbon, aligning with the national climate objectives.

Yet, despite our efforts, many in our industry are starting to ask if we are moving too slowly, particularly given that we are teetering on the edge of overshooting our 1.5°C target. We consistently fail to meet even the basic criteria set by Building Regulations, with our performance gap (the disparity between the energy consumption predicted in the design stage of a building and the energy use in actual operation) often being greater than 50%. This was evidenced in the 300 residences examined in both the Zero Carbon Hub inspection spanning 2012 to 2016 and the Innovate UK Building Performance Evaluation study of 2016, where none of the inspected homes met their anticipated standards. The vast majority fell short of compliance with Part L and Part F of the Building Regulations by a substantial margin – more than 50%![3] Have we grown so accustomed to the word 'sustainable' that it no longer effectively elicits the urgency required to initiate meaningful change? Is this word 'sustainable' starting to lose its impact and instead is being hijacked by those who would use greenwashing and virtue signalling as compliance? As we strive to achieve net-zero emissions, we must examine our overuse of the term 'sustainable'. The fact is that despite a track record of over 50 years, 'sustainable design' may have moved us along the path to better, but it has not made the substantial progress required to prevent further environmental degradation and climate change, as evidenced by our consistent, and increasingly frequent, extreme weather. The growing urgency of climate change, biodiversity loss and resource depletion has made it clear that merely sustaining current conditions is no longer sufficient.

On another level, many of you reading this book will remember the definition of sustainability as 'meeting the needs of the present without compromising the ability of future generations to meet their own needs', as popularised by the United Nations Brundtland Commission in 1987.[4] While the definition at the time included environmental, social and economic impacts, over the last 30 plus years our industry has focused heavily on the 'environmental'. This focus on the environmental aspect is understandable, not least given an increased global awareness of environmental issues including climate change, deforestation and the loss of biodiversity. The urgency of these issues propelled environmental sustainability to the forefront. Additionally, the scientific evidence of environmental degradation has had a visible and dramatic impact globally, from melting ice caps to extreme weather events.

Policy and regulatory frameworks have prioritised environmental aspects by setting measurable targets, such as net-zero carbon emissions. Global agreements, such as the Kyoto Protocol and the Paris Agreement, have placed significant emphasis on environmental targets, influencing national policies and, by extension, sustainable design. Technological advancements have also played a role. The last few decades have seen significant advancements in 'green building' technologies, making it easier and more cost-effective to implement environmentally sustainable practices, with these often being simpler to measure and quantify (e.g. energy use, carbon footprint, u-values) compared with social or economic impacts, making them a more straightforward target for improvement.

The heavy emphasis on environmental sustainability has led to an imbalance, with social and economic aspects having not been given equal consideration. This has resulted in solutions that might be environmentally sound but may not adequately address social equity or economic viability. That said, in more recent years, sustainable design has begun to evolve to encompass a more holistic view, where environmental, social and economic sustainability are integrated. Perhaps now is the time for a regenerative approach to be explored in more depth, not only to reduce harm but also to positively enhance and restore our environmental, social and economic balance.

Could this be a time for small architectural practices to step up? After all, we are part of a generation that is increasingly coming forward to challenge the status quo. This growing movement is evident in the Extinction Rebellion protests across London, the global Black Lives Matter movement sparked by the tragic murder of George Floyd, the 'me too' Movement initiated by activist Tarana Burke and the UK-wide strikes by public service bodies, including train services and NHS workers in 2022 and 2023. With the UK's commitment to aggressive climate targets, including achieving net-zero carbon emissions by 2050, the architecture industry needs to adopt more proactive and progressive strategies. Could taking a regenerative approach to how we practice architecture be the great equaliser for who gets to practice architecture too?

SUSTAINABLE AND REGENERATIVE

While sustainable and regenerative approaches are related concepts and often overlap in certain areas, they are not exactly the same.

In our introductory chapter, we looked at the difference between sustainable and regenerative design and development, and highlighted a regenerative path as the most useful one in terms of grasping the complexity of our planet and responding appropriately. Sustainability is focused on simply reducing human activities' harm to the planet. Regenerative development goes beyond reducing harm by actively seeking to restore and revitalize natural systems through innovative and restorative practices.

So, what does this look like in practice? Regenerative practices involve shifting from doing less bad to doing more good, by restoring ecosystems and biodiversity in the process. This means engaging in restorative practices, like soil regeneration, halting and reversing diminishing biodiversity and embracing energy-efficient building designs that consider factors such as water runoff and air quality.

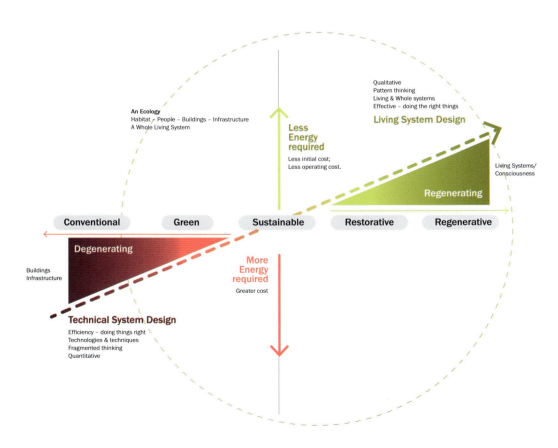

Fig 3.2 Trajectory of ecological design, source: Bill Reed, Regenesis Group

CASE STUDY

PROJECT PROFILE: BRATTLEBORO FOOD CO-OP

REGENERATIVE PRACTICE: AN INTEGRATED ECO-SYSTEM

We spoke with Bill Reed, principal of Regenesis Group in the United States, a world leader in the field of regenerative development. Reed often speaks about our integration with 'living systems', that is, the importance of seeing buildings and developments not just as standalone structures, but as integrated parts of a living system. This perspective shifts the focus from merely reducing harm to actively participating in, and contributing to, the health of ecological and social systems.

The Regenesis team embarked on a project with a grocery store in Brattleboro, Vermont, US. Established in 1975, the Brattleboro Food Co-op began as a pioneering small cooperative buying club. It has since evolved into a 14,580 square foot natural food market, serving the wider Brattleboro area. This community-owned cooperative focuses on both making local food accessible and educating the community about it. The Co-op sought Regenesis's expertise during its expansion phase to construct a new building adhering to Leadership in Energy and Environmental Design (LEED) standards. The Co-op, a significant local entity, aimed for the building to embody its principles and serve as a benchmark in energy efficiency and sustainable construction.

Through their research, Regenesis found that, in the United States, food typically travels an average of 3,600 miles before reaching its final destination. This discovery led to further questioning: what would happen if there was a truckers' strike? Or if a large supermarket chain opened in town? They realised that such events could potentially put the Brattleboro Co-op out of business within a year.

To counteract this vulnerability, the team proposed a design that would support the local food system. Regenesis and the Brattleboro Co-op worked together to structure the store to also serve as a hub for teaching community members how to prepare nutritious food and also to educate them about the impact their food choices have on the environment and their health. To accommodate the parents attending these learning sessions, the Co-op made available their longstanding children's playroom. By championing local agriculture, the Co-op could drastically reduce energy consumption compared with what the building itself would use, thereby reinforcing both their own and the community's resilience and prosperity.

As a result of this collaboration, the 100-year plan of the Brattleboro Co-op incorporated this systems-thinking approach in all their future building projects. All these transformative actions stemmed from an understanding and engagement with an existing system – a strategy not typically undertaken by many architects, but one that has the potential to inspire significant and impactful change.

Nearly a half a century in, the Co-op is now an anchor of downtown Brattleboro, functioning as a regional food system hub, enhancing community access to wholesome local food and supporting regional farmers. The four-storey edifice houses a 14,580 square foot natural food market and deli, along with the cooperative's offices, a commissary kitchen and cookery-class space. The building features rooftop solar panels and an innovative heating system that recycles heat from in-store refrigeration. More than just an eco-friendly and cooperative structure, this building embodies and continually rejuvenates the Co-op's commitment to community engagement and a robust local food ecosystem, supporting its 9,000 plus members.

Fig 3.3 Exterior view, Brattleboro Food Co-op, Vermont. The building exemplifies the Co-op's commitment to community engagement

Fig 3.4 Interior view, Brattleboro Food Co-op, Vermont. The interior reflects the Co-op's dedication to a strong local food ecosystem

It is important to note that in the UK we do not yet have many examples of full regenerative design: where every aspect of the project chimes with the requirements of regenerative design. But as British-American urbanist and writer, Sarah Ichioka, and Michael Pawlyn, director of regenerative architecture consultancy, point out in their book, *Flourish*, we must begin to adopt regenerative approaches within each project now.[5] Rather than waiting for when we might have the right client, with the right budget and the right altruistic intentions to implement regenerative principles, we should find opportunities for win-win scenarios right now. From creating diverse teams to designing buildings that co-evolve with nature, the opportunities are there when we choose to look for them. Over time, this series of smaller interventions will begin to pull together to trigger the necessary paradigm shift.

Architecture Today and UK Architects Declare have helpfully launched a Regenerative Architecture Index (RAI).[6] The aim of the RAI is to establish a standard for assessing the advancement of practices towards regenerative principles in both practice and projects. It acknowledges the imperative for a built environment that goes beyond mitigating negative effects to actively fostering positive impacts for the present and future.

> The RAI is built on a framework incorporating three key criteria:
>
> **1. Being a good ancestor:** This concerns a transition in mindset within practices to embrace genuinely long-term perspectives. Our present choices must account for seven generations to come, prioritising adaptability and flexibility for the future. Achieving this demands innovative thinking, as existing models fall short of long-term benefits.
>
> **2. Co-evolving with nature:** This emphasises our interconnectedness with nature, as integral components of living systems rather than entities detached from them. Our endeavours ought to actively contribute to the regeneration of ecosystems by drawing inspiration from, and collaborating with, natural systems. Achieving this entails designing with circularity in mind and promoting closed-loop energy, material and water cycles.
>
> **3. Creating a just space for people:** This underscores the importance of facilitating social cohesion, economic empowerment and overall well-being for everyone. Our design methodologies should cultivate a collective sense of responsibility, enabling communities to self-organise and enhance their resilience. Achieving this necessitates employing ethical, inclusive and participatory approaches.

Arguably the first small steps are in the questions we ask ourselves when approaching our design work: what will thinking more regeneratively look like? And how will this play out in our practice? Below are some examples we have gathered, which you may find useful for shifting your mindset.

Ask questions differently: Every architectural project exists within a system that includes a variety of elements: the natural environment, the community, local regulations, available materials and technologies, among others. A co-evolutionary process explores where human systems and natural systems evolve together in a mutually beneficial way. This approach involves understanding and working with the dynamics of a place, including its culture, ecology and economy.

Adopt a whole-system design: Adopting a regenerative approach emphasises the significance of whole-system thinking in design. This approach goes beyond sustainable practices that often focus on individual elements (like energy efficiency or water conservation) to consider the entire system – including social, cultural, ecological and economic aspects.

Potential-based design: Instead of focusing solely on solving problems, as many of us architects have been taught to do for so long, regenerative development focuses on realising the potential of a place. This means understanding and nurturing the inherent capabilities of an environment, community and ecosystem to thrive and evolve.

Educational role: Over the coming years and decades, architects, planners, developers and all others involved in the built environment will need to be educated about systems thinking and the principles of regenerative design to create truly sustainable communities.

Collaborative and inclusive process: Regenerative development requires a collaborative approach that includes stakeholders from various sectors (e.g. community members, ecologists, anthropologist, economists and others), ensuring that the development is truly beneficial for all involved.

Fig 3.5 The LBC standard, based on information from the IFLI

Strategies for regenerative design have begun to be codified by various bodies. The International Living Future Institute is an organisation based in the United States that has set itself up as a holistic, sustainable design standard and has developed the Living Building Challenge (LBC). It's widely considered one of the most rigorous building standards in the world, focusing not only on environmental performance but also on social and community aspects. The LBC encourages the creation of spaces that are self-sufficient, promote the health of their occupants and have a positive impact on the environment around them.

Growing in popularity in the UK is the WELL Building Standard, a performance-based system for measuring, certifying and monitoring features of the built environment that impact human health and well-being. Developed by the International WELL Building Institute, this standard focuses on enhancing occupants' health and well-being through the built environment.

Both of these organisations include a certification process for their buildings.

Diving a little more into the LBC, the standard is structured around seven performance areas, or 'petals': place, water, energy, health and happiness, materials, equity and beauty. Each petal is subdivided into specific imperatives that buildings must meet to achieve certification. LBC buildings are designed to meet all water needs through captured precipitation or closed-loop water systems and must purify wastewater on site (net positive water). LBC places an emphasis on responsible materials – using non-toxic, sustainable and locally sourced materials.

Buildings are to generate more energy than they consume (net positive energy), typically achieved through renewable energy sources like solar panels. This might be where a well-known standard such as Passivhaus comes into play. As the adoption of Passivhaus expands across the UK and Europe, certain projects are advancing beyond the basic Passivhaus criteria to achieve net-zero objectives. Besides the traditional 'Passivhaus Classic', there are the 'Passivhaus Plus' and 'Passivhaus Premium' categories, which incorporate renewable energy generation into their certification requirements. Passivhaus Plus buildings significantly reduce their energy consumption and simultaneously generate as much energy as they use. Passivhaus Premium goes a step further, with buildings substantially producing more energy than they need for operation.

CASE STUDY

PROJECT PROFILE: CUERDEN VALLEY PARK VISITOR CENTRE

The Cuerden Valley Park visitor centre in Preston, Lancashire, stands as a great example of regenerative design. It is the first LBC registered building in the UK, designed by architect Barbara Jones and designer Jakub Wihan of Straw Works.

At the beginning of the project, the client's request for an 'eco building' initiated a journey into understanding the LBC and the use of natural, regenerative materials. Central to the design concept was community involvement, aligning the project with its setting in the park and embedding LBC's guiding principles using regenerative materials.

The visitor centre is built using plant-based materials, targeting net-zero carbon throughout its lifecycle. The material selection is intentionally minimal: a wooden framework filled with straw, coated in lime plaster and complemented by natural finishes, including natural linoleum flooring, linseed oil-based sealants and natural paints. The architect's long-standing commitment to avoiding cement is evident here, with the centre resting on foundations of timber and recycled car tyres filled with compacted stone. The building's construction methods are visible and straightforward, allowing even those without building experience to participate in the construction process.

The project was a finalist in the 2020 Alliance for Sustainable Building Products awards, garnering particular praise for its high level of community involvement in both design and construction, which fostered a strong sense of ownership.

Fig 3.6 Cuerden Valley Park visitor centre

CASE STUDY

PRACTICE PROFILE: COLLECTIVE WORKS

REGENERATIVE FRAMEWORKS: INTEGRATIVE DESIGN PROCESSES

Established in 2012, London-based architecture and design studio, Collective Works, is fuelled with ambition to design beautiful spaces with an awareness of their responsibility to the planet, to society and to each other. Collective Works are a small practice of eight people, including three directors, who specialise in a range of sectors including housing and healthcare, small domestic, community and education.

Alasdair Dixon, a director at Collective Works, observed that one of the key reasons for their joining industry bodies such as UK Architects Declare and being a part of the RIBA Ethics and Sustainable Development Commission was a recognition that the climate challenge couldn't be addressed within the four walls of their small practice alone; there was a need to share their knowledge and gain expertise, as well as to understand how their own work is positioned within the broader industry.

Dixon acknowledged that social impact and social value were missing components of many projects in the industry, particularly in the light of the 2019 IPCC Report, which highlighted the interconnected nature of environmental and social concerns.[7] In 2019, Collective Works signed up to UK Architects Declare and in 2021 they joined the RIBA 2030 Climate Challenge.

In taking strong action and making a commitment to measure their own personal carbon footprint, Collective Works joined the Better Futures scheme, an accelerator programme offering free expert advice to support clean-tech, low-carbon businesses. Following this, the practice decided they needed to go further. They chose to develop their own baseline of what sustainable development looks like to them, and decided that every client they work with would have this standard applied, irrespective of what had been asked for. Targets are project specific as they work up to what a minimum baseline looks like across all projects. They defined nine categories of responsible and beautiful projects. These are: emotive, harmonious, considered, nurture well-being, connected to nature, participatory, low carbon, ethical and evaluated (all projects are evaluated after completion and once they are being used).

When working on healthcare projects, they have adopted a 'social prescribing' approach. This means ensuring citizens are healthy not only physically, through medication, treatments and operations, but mentally, through additional services such as community groups, gardening sessions, yoga classes or even access to financial advice services. This perspective allows designers in the built environment to provide additional space for softer services that positively impact well-being.

Collective Works have experienced some challenges: sometimes clients are open to implementing carbon embodied principles and sometimes they are not. This is something many small practices face, and which ultimately encourages us to think about how we communicate the implications of ignoring issues that concern our environment. Education is key. There are still huge gaps in our knowledge and becoming carbon literate while avoiding carbon tunnel vision is a challenge.

As Dixon observes: 'Carbon is the metric but not at the expense of biodiversity, social value and beauty.'

Fig 3.7 Collective Works directors, Khuzema Hussain, Siri Zanelli and Alasdair Ben Dixon

Fig 3.8 Rise project. A unique 200-seat temporary theatre for the show Rise, which captured Londoners' hopes and fears for the environment

As small practices whose clients are just about getting to grips with sustainability, and with some only able to move the needle when the government's Future Building Standard comes to bear, how can we start to explore some of the key aspects delivered by a regenerative framework such as the LBC? What if we committed ourselves to a new baseline performance standard that is higher and more far-reaching than previous targets? Existing performance targets such as RIBA 2030, LETI targets and Passivhaus could form the new baseline, with stretch targets pointing towards the LBC or indeed our own frameworks. Could we choose to radically rethink what is possible, based on what we know is required for people and the planet? Or, asked another way, can we afford not to?

> Here are some pointers that may help you in implementing your own regenerative framework. These have the potential to take your practice above and beyond current guidance and hopefully pave the way for further, and more effective, change:
>
> **Education and training:** Staff should be knowledgeable about sustainable design principles and building physics as a baseline. Consider training or workshops focused on the LBC standard. Educate clients about the benefits of LBC, including environmental, health and potential financial advantages. We also encourage architects to commit to taking courses that will challenge their thinking specifically in regenerative and sustainability leadership; courses such as the UKGBC Future Leaders course, the Regenesis Practitioner course and the Better Futures programme. The opportunities are plenty and only with a serious commitment can we start making key changes in our industry.
>
> **Early integration in the design process:** Sustainable design elements should be integrated from the earliest stages of the design process. This might involve more upfront planning but leads to greater long-term benefits.
>
> **Collaboration with specialised consultants:** For small practices, collaborating with other experts in areas like renewable energy, water management and sustainable materials can be valuable. Invite speakers within these areas to come into your office and share their expertise with colleagues and encourage clients to seek their advice too.
>
> **Pilot projects:** Start with small-scale projects to gain experience and showcase capabilities in sustainable design.
>
> **Cost–benefit analysis:** This should encompass not only financial costs, but carbon and environmental costs too. Depending on the scope and scale of a scheme, capital costs for more sustainable builds are coming down and, when put in the context of operational costs and savings, better decisions can be made. Providing clients with a detailed cost-benefit analysis can help in decision making.
>
> **Commit to going further:** Some questions we can ask ourselves, our teams and our business:
> 1. What new commitments can we implement now to start putting regenerative practice into action?
> 2. Who will I/we need to bring along the journey and how will we convince them to come on board?
> 3. What small action can I/we implement now?

THE REQUREMENT FOR RETROFIT
We cannot speak about regenerative development without addressing our retrofit challenge. Retrofitting homes brings us the opportunity to restore and renew the UK's existing building stock. With 80% of the homes we will need in 2050 already built, we can stay focused on unearthing the inherent potential of existing infrastructure and ensure that any responses add value to our heritage – breathing new life into structures to ensure another 60, 100 or even 150 years of service to humankind. Approximately 29 million homes will need to be retrofitted over the next 25 plus years and upgrading the nation's homes represents one of the biggest opportunities the UK has to reduce carbon emissions while tackling the cost-of-living crisis, energy security, green jobs and a more equitable workforce.[8]

Small practices are uniquely placed to take advantage of this opportunity, not least because of the sheer scale of the challenge – 29 million homes await. To step up to this challenge we will need to upskill ourselves in the face of the nuanced retrofit challenges highlighted below. Additionally, because the government has offered homeowners various schemes and incentives to decarbonise their homes, small practices – where 60% to 80% of revenue comes from private housing – can help clients in a more holistic way including directing them to funding opportunities.[9] Incentives range from boiler upgrade schemes (government allocation of £1.5 billion) to grants towards heat pumps and warm home discount schemes, including wall and loft insulation. Adding to this, small practices often have niche expertise including historical building conservation, Passivhaus standards, or use of specific sustainable materials that can be aligned with retrofit projects. With a growing awareness among homeowners about the benefits of energy efficiency – partly driven by rising energy costs – practices are seeing a change in the briefs we receive: no longer are design considerations the only things being requested; critically, more energy-efficient homes are being required.

In what is being heralded in the industry as a watershed moment and a turning point for our climate crisis, the Secretary of State, Michael Gove, stepped-in to block Marks & Spencer from demolition in July 2023, following a proposal from developers to build a new 'sustainable' building on the site of the iconic flagship store on Oxford Street. This story captured the imagination of those beyond the architecture industry, prompting people to question if this might set a precedent in favour of retention, or else lead to confusion across our industry over what is deemed 'sustainable'.

What is clear is that we will need all hands to the pump, and this means small practices actively lobbying national government for a national upgrade programme – something the UKGBC has already called for. Without immediate and national action our buildings will persist in wasting valuable and costly heat, which escapes through every uninsulated wall, roof and door. Small practices will need to work with local government to provide guidance and support for local retrofit programmes. This presents a big opportunity to small practices in particular, where local authorities are specifically looking to work with small and medium-sized businesses as part of their social value commitments.

Retrofitting our homes will be complex and poses a significant challenge. To execute it effectively, we must embrace systemic thinking and regenerative approaches. This means avoiding linear, one-dimensional decision-making approaches that could inadvertently worsen the lives of the people who interact with our buildings and have a negative impact on the planet. An example might be installing internal wall insulation in a heritage building that requires stopping that insulation at the coving detail level, thereby potentially causing thermal bridging at the uninsulated area. This will, in turn, lead to an eventual degradation of the building structure. Without a thorough grasp of the complex ecosystems involved, well-intentioned retrofit interventions may exacerbate issues like condensation, dampness and mould, resulting in deteriorated living conditions for occupants and rendering buildings uninhabitable. As we move into the next few decades of deep retrofits, we are once again positioned to influence our environment substantially. It is therefore imperative for us to embrace approaches that don't lead people to have a worse quality of life post-retrofit.

Retrofit is complex because we are dealing with existing properties on multiple scales. Be it individual homes that have had modern extensions or interventions; or working with a series of housing association assets that have not been cared for over the years; or indeed the heritage properties across the country that will need special attention. In addition to this, the ownership structure is a mix of private residential and social housing. The vast majority of existing properties are detached, semi-detached and terraced homes, all requiring a slightly different approach. And while two homes might look the same from the outside, understanding occupier use and undertaking a deep retrofit assessment will be necessary to understand how best to deal with each property.

Again, small practices are uniquely placed to undertake retrofit projects, due to their share of the residential market, but also their ability and willingness to take on smaller, more bespoke projects with a particular attention to detail.

PAS 2035 and the retrofit coordinator role
The quality of retrofits of social housing already outstrips that of the private sector, with the average Energy Performance Certificate (EPC) rating across all social rent housing types at 70, followed by private rent and owner-occupiers at 66 and 64 respectively.[10] This is because the government has set a target for all social homes to reach a minimum EPC 'C' by 2030, and will only fund these works where agreed Public Sector Decarbonisation Schemes (PSDS) are adopted (i.e. the Social Housing Decarbonisation Fund (SHDF) and the Low Skills Decarbonisation Fund (LSDF), among others).[11] Our industry will find a growing need for architects to become involved in Heat Decarbonisation Plans (HDPs) for public sector bodies. Even with the barriers to retrofit, including a lack of funding, policy certainty, ability/skill in the supply chain and time, this external driver for change will mean significant change for architects too.[12]

At present there is a dearth of retrofit specialists. There are currently under 3,000 retrofit coordinators with a forecasted 50,000 required by 2030,[13] and over 4,200 needed to support delivery across London alone.[14] The need for a deep understanding of the retrofit process, and its impact on people and planet, will require many more architects to retrain in this area. With a significant gap in knowledge of building physics, this training is indeed critical. Not only this, for architects to remain competitive and collaborative, the necessity for retraining will also continue to grow as the retrofit coordination role is open to all disciplines in the construction field (contractors, builders, project managers and housing asset managers, among others).

Initially released in 2019, PAS 2035 represents the UK's benchmark for the retrofitting of residential properties and the resulting roles of retrofit coordinator and retrofit designer.[15] PAS 2035 was published following the 'Each Home Counts' review in 2018, which uncovered systemic failures and poor standards in retrofitted properties across the country.[16] Homes that were insulated and made more airtight were not provided with adequate ventilation, leading to issues such as damp, mould and condensation – issues that had a negative effect on the quality of life of the occupiers, and which are expensive to address. As a result, many architects will need to become conversant with stock condition surveys, Improvement Option Evaluations (IOEs) and Medium-Term Improvement Plans (MTIPs).

Fig 3.9 Typical UK home showing mould growth from interstitial condensation. This is cleaned down each year by the homeowner

The core principles of PAAS 2035 explained

A set of core principles underpin PAS 2035. These are often mistaken for jargon and it is crucial that your business develops a thorough understanding of these.

Fig 3.10 The core principles of PAS 2035 explained

PAS 2035 details the management and execution of retrofit projects, and the PAS 2035 course is now delivered by a host of organisations across the UK including The Retrofit Academy, AECB and others, who deliver a diploma-level course in a rigorous 12-week programme. Compliance with PAS 2035 is mandatory for any retrofit projects that require government funding. Small practices can explore PAS 2035 not only to address the domestic market, but also for a wider remit including affordable housing. In 2023 the government allocated £1.25 billion (the third round of government funding) to the SHDF to enable the insulation and retrofitting of up to 140,000 social homes (to EPC 'C').[17] This need to retrofit our existing stock presents an opportunity for small practices to be involved in bigger projects that are often reserved for larger practices who sit in strategic positions providing business insights to clients, writing briefs and developing retrofit programmes.[18] Being part of a retrofit revolution allows small practices – whose workloads typically comprise a greater proportion of housing projects – to deliver on the detail, using our intimate knowledge of building retrofits and expertise in building physics to contribute meaningfully to addressing retrofit at scale.[19] With 29 million homes requiring retrofitting by 2050, all hands are needed.

Key roles have come out of the PAS 2035 requirement, among these are the retrofit assessor, retrofit designer and retrofit coordinator, with the latter taking a holistic view across a retrofit programme. An architect can train in any of these roles. The retrofit coordinator role is a crucial component in the PAS 2035 standard and is central to ensuring that this process is carried out correctly and sustainably. The main duties of a retrofit coordinator include recognising, evaluating and handling both technical and procedural risks typically linked to domestic retrofit initiatives. Their responsibilities encompass supervising the planning, detailing and follow-up monitoring and assessment of energy-saving measures, all in alignment with the PAS 2035 standards.

CASE STUDY

PRACTICE PROFILE: GBOLADE DESIGN STUDIO

REGENERATIVE RETROFIT: HILL HOUSE

Hill House is located on a private site in a conservation area. The clients were looking to address the issues of overheating in the summer months and freezing conditions in winter months brought on by a series of ad hoc and unsympathetic extensions, bolted on to the original property over a series of years.

Fig 3.11 A redesign and deep retrofit of a home in a conservation area to LETI retrofit 'best practice' standards, Gbolade Design Studio

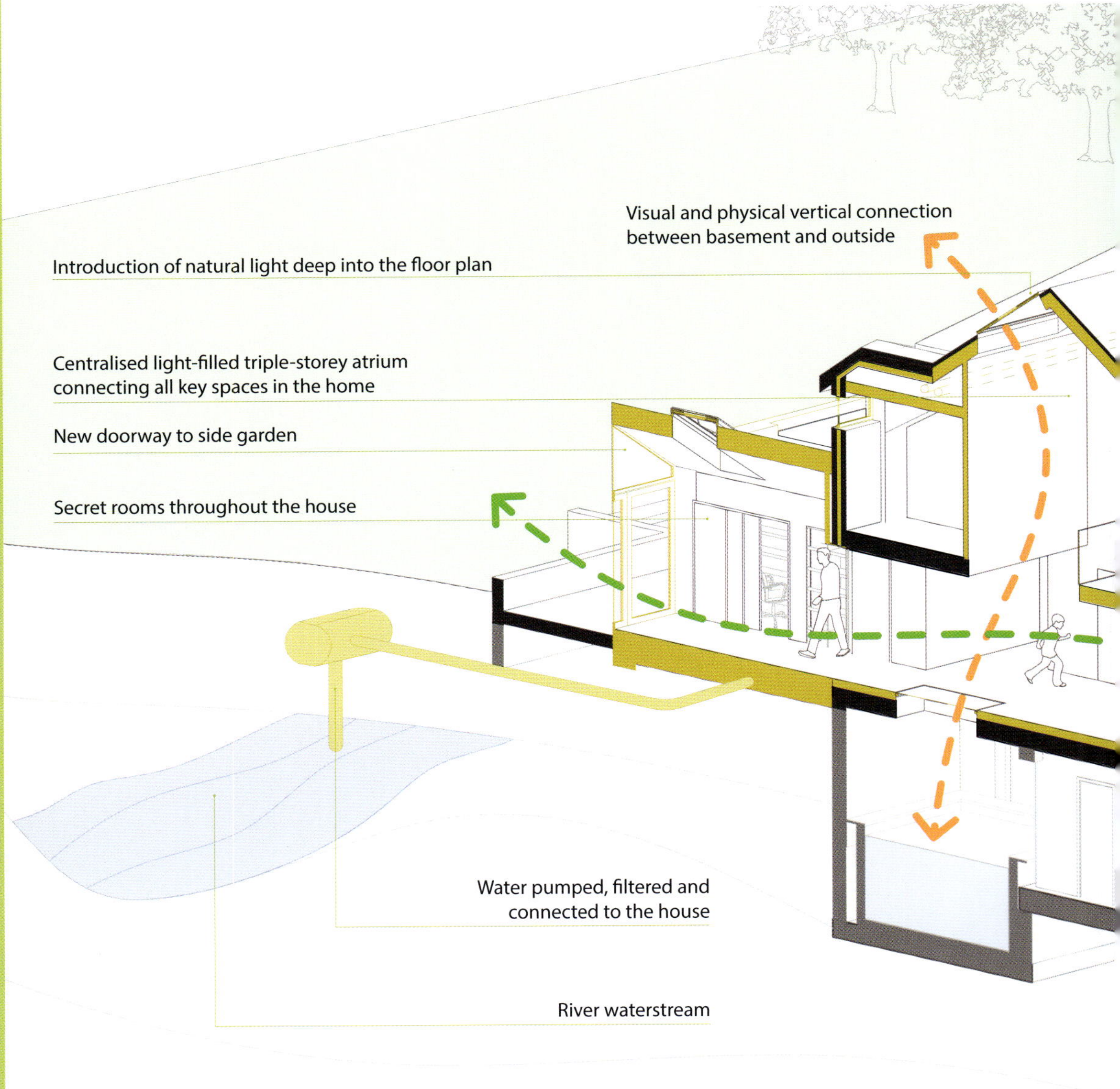

CHANGING THE GAME

Visual and physical vertical connection between basement and outside

Introduction of natural light deep into the floor plan

Centralised light-filled triple-storey atrium connecting all key spaces in the home

New doorway to side garden

Secret rooms throughout the house

Water pumped, filtered and connected to the house

River waterstream

Fig 3.12 Design approach showing retrofit provisions including material reuse and visual and physical connections between internal spaces and with the outside world

CHAPTER 3　　　　　　ENVIRONMENTAL REGENERATION　　　　　　　　　　　　　　**61**

Atrium wall lined with natural material

New suspended and cantilevered feature staircase

Existing roof retained and retrofitted with new insulation

Existing building fabric retained and retrofitted using internal wall insulation

New recessed entrance lined with timber slats

Existing windows refurbished using high-performance triple glazing

Visual and physical connection from driveway to rear garden

EMBODIED CARBON APPROACH

Low- and zero-carbon report was undertaken at design stage with a focus on lowering embodied carbon and operational energy

Structure
The existing building is retained almost in its entirety. New structural elements major with timber unless steel was critical to use

Windows and doors
Specified from European suppliers with renewable energy as main energy generation. Aluminium-timber composites to reduce long-term maintenance

Technologies
- Smart controls are used for occupant control and reduction of energy use
- Low-energy lighting
- Underfloor heating

Rainwater harvesting
Collected using water butts

Foundations and building weight
The existing foundations were retained and reused

Circular economy approach
Where the old conservatory had to be removed due to overheating in summer and freezing conditions in winter, the brickwork was reused in other parts of the building. The old parquet flooring has been carefully removed, cleaned, and reused as the swivel door to the new Snug Room

Fig 3.13 Sustainability approach for retrofitted property including embodied carbon approach and operational energy approach

OPERATIONAL ENERGY APPROACH

Energy use intensity target: < 60 kWh/m²/yr
Space heating demand design target: 25kWh/m²/yr

Renewable energy
20% of roof coverage with average solar PV of 14kWh/m²/yr

Roofs
Existing roof retained with low embodied carbon mineral wool insulation
Timber rafters retained
Roof U-value: 0.12W/m²K. Rooflights U-value: 0.70W/m²K

External wall
Cavity and internal wall insulation
High-performing low embodied carbon mineral wool insulation
Wall U-value: 0.15-0.18W/m²K

Overheating
New portico roof extension to provide shade
Window positioning and sizing to ensure no overheating

Windows and doors
Existing windows replaced with new triple-glazed windows and doors
U-value: 0.9 w/m²K
Glass G-value to achieve 0.5-0.6

Airtightness 3.0 ach@50Pa
Thermal bridging 0.07 Ψ-value
Ventilation MVHR

Ground floor
New insulation above existing ground floor slab.
U-value: 0.15 W/m²K

Renewable energy
Renewable energy generation for heating and hot water achieved using a ground source heat pump

The environmental response is a deep retrofit, designed to be sustainable and regenerative in its approach. This project embodies the principles of a circular economy by retaining and retrofitting the existing home to achieve LETI retrofit best practice targets for a 'constrained' building – i.e. one within a conservation area. The building fabric has been retained, with materials from elements that were demolished, such as the old conservatory and original parquet flooring, recycled and reused. Walls, roofs and floors have been insulated, existing materials reused and the home is fossil-fuel free, using renewables such as a ground source heat pump and solar panels to address energy needs.

With its improved airtightness, the home now incorporates a mechanical ventilation with heat recovery (MVHR) system that provides fresh clean air and a comfortable internal environment.

Energy consumption was reduced by designing to extremely low fabric U-values ranging between 0.12 and 0.18 W/m^{2}K. Cavity-wall and internal-wall insulation was applied to walls, above ground insulation to floor slabs and loft insulation to roofs. Thermal bridging and airtightness were addressed with careful detailing around the junctions. Mineral wool insulation was chosen over carbon-intensive polyisocyanurate (PIR) insulation. Moisture risk and thermal bridge assessments were undertaken in-house to ensure good surface temperatures above 17 °C, reducing the chance for condensation, damp and mould growth post retrofit.

New rooflights were cleverly positioned on east-facing roof pitches to maximise daylight while avoiding overheating. The home is fossil-fuel free, using renewable sources such as solar panels to provide energy, with any over-production of electricity returned to the National Grid. While the site has incredible biodiversity, new green roofs are being installed to enhance this.

Post construction, the home has been assessed and awarded an EPC 'B', an improvement on the pre-retrofit EPC 'D' rating with the assessor highlighting this is the 'best performing home he has measured in over 15 years'. Furthermore, with clear intention from the client, this build contributed positively to businesses that were local, female-led, minority-led or small and medium-sized enterprises (SMEs).

Figs 3.14,15 Hill House, views of the final retrofitted home

Figs 3.16 Hill House, kitchen view showing skylight

Retrofit and health

At the end of 2022, the Institute of Health Equity published a report titled 'Fuel Poverty, Cold Homes and Health Inequalities in the UK', in which they highlighted the impact of the quality of our homes on our health and well-being.[20] In 2023, the government announced that the Social Housing Regulations Bill would incorporate Awaab's Law, forcing social landlords to fix damp and mould within a strict time limit.[21] This law was brought about following the tragic death of two-year-old Awaab Ishak, caused by the damp and mould in his home.

Although you might be aware that our homes affect our health, it is worth taking a closer look at some of the impacts of living in cold and damp homes. Fuel-poor households can lead to poor mental health, with babies, children and older people being the most vulnerable.[22] Cold homes stunt early development in children and can lead to poor education: crucial early years are adversely affected as babies living in colder temperatures require more calories for growth.[23] Cold temperatures weaken resistance to respiratory infections, leading to conditions like bronchiolitis and asthma, exacerbated by condensation, damp and mould, with respiratory illnesses twice as likely in children from these environments. Moreover, asthma worsens with each degree drop in indoor temperature.[24] Children's mental health is also impacted, with higher rates of negative symptoms in children and increased maternal depression due to added stress and discomfort, contributing to anxiety and depression.[25] Furthermore, children's education is affected, as energy-inefficient homes lead to more school absences due to illnesses from damp and mould, as well as difficulty studying in colder homes, leading to UK children missing more school days than their EU counterparts.[26]

For adults, cold temperatures can lead to circulatory problems and exacerbate long-term conditions including dementia. Cold homes can lower resistance to respiratory infections and worsen conditions like asthma and chronic obstructive pulmonary disease (COPD). Circulatory issues arise as cold temperatures increase blood pressure and blood viscosity, increasing the risk of heart attacks and strokes. For older people, cold exacerbates health risks due to less effective thermoregulation.[27]

Fig 3.17 Grahame Park project, Barnet, Gbolade Design Studio. Regeneration of this space prioritised pedestrian movement across the site and maximising opportunities for natural overlooking and shared play

On the other end of the scale, homes that overheat (that is an internal temperature above 25°C for living rooms and 26°C for bedrooms, for more than 1% of the hours in a year) can lead to heat exhaustion and heatstroke. Prolonged exposure might be characterised by symptoms such as dizziness, fatigue and nausea as the body's temperature regulation fails. A common symptom of overheating that a surprising number of us tolerate is disturbance to sleep, even if we know that poor sleep can often have a cascading effect on overall health, impacting mood, cognitive function and physical health. And finally, prolonged exposure to uncomfortable temperatures can lead to increased stress, irritability and, in some cases, can exacerbate mental health conditions like anxiety and depression.[28]

Today we have more of an understanding around the link between our health and well-being and the quality of our homes, and upgrading and retrofitting existing buildings must become our default position. Energy efficiency interventions improve health and well-being outcomes associated with cold homes and retrofitting houses improves thermal comfort while reducing carbon emissions. A well-known example of a large-scale retrofit is Peabody's Thamesmead Estate regeneration. This involved a comprehensive approach to address severe issues of condensation, damp and mould in their housing stock. The initiative aimed to ensure that the properties provided safe and healthy living conditions while reducing costs associated with condensation, damp and mould for both residents and the landlord. The project began with identifying the root causes of these issues (inadequate ventilation, poor insulation and outdated heating systems) and developing a coordinated strategy to implement long-term solutions.

Technological interventions were central to this strategy. Peabody installed 145 Switchee units across various homes. These smart devices monitored temperature, humidity and airflow, allowing for precise identification of properties most at risk and assessing the effectiveness of different interventions. Multiple retrofit solutions, including Aereco demand-controlled mechanical extract ventilation (MEV) systems, were tested. The real-time data from the Switchee units ensured only effective measures were implemented, avoiding unnecessary and costly interventions.[29] The results were significant, with an estimated annual reduction of 26.4 tonnes of carbon dioxide and a 15% decrease in heating bills for residents. The retrofit effectively resolved condensation, damp and mould issues, leading to improved living conditions and substantial long-term remedial cost savings for Peabody, estimated at £219,000.[30]

In addition to these technological solutions, Peabody enhanced their approach by establishing a dedicated damp, mould and condensation team, improving case management processes, and conducting proactive reviews and audits of high-risk properties. These steps ensured that issues were addressed promptly and effectively, and residents received the necessary support throughout the process.[31] This comprehensive and strategic approach highlights the effectiveness of using coordinated efforts to tackle significant housing issues, benefiting both residents and the housing provider.

To avoid the risks associated with a retrofit, adopting a whole-house retrofit approach is key. This involves taking into consideration the fabric of a building – walls, roofs, floors – alongside ventilation, overheating and airtightness, and being careful not to propose single-measure options (such as insulation alone or changing windows alone) without considering the unintended consequences that may arise. Alongside a formalised retrofit course, the Sustainable Traditional Buildings Alliance (STBA) has an online guidance wheel that is incredibly useful to practitioners looking to gain an understanding of how one measure might interact with other measures for a retrofit.

Fig 3.18 Gbolade Design Studio's whole-house retrofit plan. These are produced for each specific project taking into consideration the requirements of that project

EMBRACING TECHNOLOGY

The period between 2020 and 2024 has seen an explosion in how we use technology, including artificial intelligence (AI), in the architectural industry. A 2024 RIBA survey found that 43% of architects felt that AI had already improved efficiency in architectural design processes and that it will be widely adopted and integrated into practice to deliver tangible benefits in the near term.[34] Visualisation platform Midjourney launched in July 2022, followed by Stable Diffusion in August 2022, and by the end of 2023, Adobe had launched its Photoshop Beta AI image generator and well-recognised architectural tech company Graphisoft launched the built-in visualisation AI for the latest version of ArchiCAD. ChatGPT has become a research assistant in many spheres, while Reed AI takes our meeting minutes and automatically distributes them to attendees, cutting administrative time. The use of AI to improve the environmental sustainability of designs – including incorporating environmental and contextual data, providing real-time analytics and showing essential insights regarding energy use, sunlight and overheating, as well as noise and wind information – is already influencing how architects are designing, with 21% of architects already employing AI in environmental sustainability analysis, a figure that is set to grow.[35]

AI is having a significant and transformative role in architecture by providing tools and systems that assist architects and designers in creating more efficient, sustainable and environmentally responsive architecture. No longer do we need to wait to receive mechanical, electric, plumbing and heating (MEPH) calculations at RIBA Stage 2+, or Stages 3 or 4 to understand if our buildings meet the energy and ventilation requirements – potentially forcing us to redesign at a late stage, leading to costly redesign and abortive work that we will often not be paid for. Technology has allowed us to leapfrog a few stages and has invited us to adopt a more iterative way of working; to understand the operational energy and embodied carbon impact of our projects from the outset; to explore ideas more efficiently at RIBA Stage 1 with options that allow us to make smarter decisions and streamline our workflow.

Alongside visualisations, AI-powered tools are starting to shape how we produce information. Programmes like Testfit, Spacio and Finch use real-time (generative) AI configurators to undertake feasibility studies, making it easy to undertake microclimatic-specific site planning for rapid concept iterations. Tools like Cove integrate sun path analysis, embodied carbon data and operational energy, as well as highlighting the risk of overheating as part of the basic package.

Programmes like Graphisoft's ArchiCAD have enhanced their own offering too: while the 'energy evaluator' functionality has existed in the programme for years, its use has increased as a dynamic sustainability modelling tool that measures operational energy, undertakes thermal bridge assessments (including providing psi-values) and highlights the risks of overheating. We can even input fuel type and predict future energy bills in a dwelling. Plugin tools for ArchiCAD can measure embodied carbon. In other words, all the requirements for measuring the RIBA 2030 Climate Challenge targets (operational energy, embodied carbon, daylight, etc.) can be undertaken by the architect at RIBA Stages 1, 2 and 3 without leaving your building information modelling (BIM) authoring software. Taking advantage of the amount of time and resources saved, and the amounts of detailed analysis explored with better decision-making incorporated at early-stage design, changes the game.

The shift in what is now available to many small practices is immense and workflows are changing rapidly as a result. Time spent requesting quotes from Visualiser and CGI specialists has dropped significantly as architects can now get high-quality outputs from visualisation tools much quicker. Administrative tasks are becoming more streamlined as AI programmes help to schedule appointments and send out meeting minutes. Many of these tools can be used at the various RIBA stages with some more integral at differing stages.

Most significant in this change is that the usual barrier to the adoption and implementation of these advanced tools for small practices – i.e. cost – is not there. Many of the tools mentioned are either free or have a low subscription fee, removing this often-impenetrable barrier to entry. Of course, big tech does get something in return … your data. So perhaps, free purely in a financial sense, is the better phrasing.

While AI's many tools are not yet at the stage of being manipulated to obtain the minute details that might matter to an architect, we are moving there at a dizzying speed, and might do well to start implementing these tools now.

CASE STUDY

PRACTICE PROFILE: STUDIO SEARCH AND NATIONAL RETROFIT HUB

REGENERATIVE RETROFIT: A TEAM EFFORT
Studio seARCH was established in London in 2015 by Sara Edmonds and David Powis. The practice works across all London boroughs and have also completed projects in Kingston upon Thames and rural Ireland. Studio seARCH believes that architecture is about working in close partnership with clients to search for and reveal the opportunities hidden in each individual project.

Edmonds advocates for systemic change around low-carbon domestic retrofit projects. She co-founded Home Energy Action Lab (HEAL), a framework test bed for community-based domestic retrofit services, and she hosts two podcasts, *Accelerate to Zero* and her own *Zero Ambitions* podcast. Edmonds is a certified Passivhaus designer with a background of working on heritage projects. Her practice focuses on residential refurbishments and extensions, though she admits that 'there's a big chunk of me that believes we should build nothing new at all'.[32]

Edmonds observed that the teaching of building physics and systems was heavily lacking within the architecture education sector. This motivated her to pursue the training to become a Passivhaus designer. Edmonds is driven by the question of how we can get to a zero-carbon future in the built environment, and how we can facilitate that by engaging and collaborating with other sectors. In explaining her motives behind starting the *Zero Ambitions* podcast, Edmonds highlighted the crucial need for intersectionality in addressing climate, racial and social justice within the built environment. She emphasises that these aspects are inseparable and essential for achieving a zero-carbon future. The podcast focuses on exploring ways to streamline schemes and themes related to retrofitting in the built environment, while questioning industry and societal actions towards this goal. Edmonds underscored the importance of considering diverse voices in the discussion, especially given the need for retrofitting nearly 27 million homes by 2050 to meet minimum building regulations and zero-carbon targets. Indeed, to meet such targets, we would need to be retrofitting the equivalent of one home every 35 seconds between 2020 and 2050.[33]

Edmonds redefined 'retrofit' as not just an architectural challenge but also as a health issue and a social wealth-building opportunity, representing a transformative potential beyond mere insulation. Her *Zero Ambitions* podcast aims to explore these multifaceted opportunities and encourages learning from different agendas and practices. Challenging the conventional understanding of architecture, she suggests that an architect is defined more by their thought processes than by the buildings they create. She proposes using existing materials rather than continuously extracting new resources from the planet, especially considering the increasing anthropogenic mass compared with natural biomass. This perspective is part of her broader vision of reimagining retrofit as a multifaceted solution that goes beyond traditional architectural approaches.

Finally, Edmonds suggests that other small practices looking to change the business-as-usual paradigm could join networks such as the Architects Climate Action Network (ACAN) and UK Architects Declare, and implement their findings. She also advises finding common ground with clients without shutting down their ideas. She notes that it's important to 'own what you don't know' as this breaks down barriers between the client and architect and can allow for the opening up of new routes for collaboration.

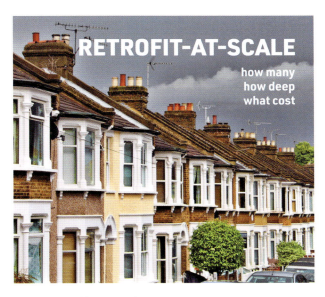

Fig 3.19 SDFoundation's 'Retrofit-At-Scale' publication

Fig 3.20 Emerging AI landscape, Arka Works AI generated CGI

Visit the Arka Works website

Carving out new roles

Every few decades an innovation asks architects to question our role in the marketplace. Never has this consideration been more pertinent than in the last two years, with such rapid advancements in technology. Social media feeds include a plethora of posts by current architecture students asking what their role might be by the time they come out of university, given the pace of change and adoption of AI technology. It is intriguing, and perhaps not surprising given the notoriously creative nature of architects, to see how practitioners are adapting to this new environment. Architects, and specifically those in small practices, are no longer waiting for the tech owners to produce the data needed for various projects. Many architects are now creating their own environmental tools, which they are either making available for free, or selling as plugins on the open market.

DesignLCA is one such tool, created by Formfaktor, a Danish company who wanted to bring change to the industry. They created and launched a free plugin that calculates life cycle assessments for a building. The process works off ArchiCAD's dynamic energy modelling and includes environmental product datasheet (EPD) data, which the designer can manipulate for specific products. Another example is a German practice that has built a condensation analysis plugin to ArchiCAD that visualises likely dew points. Yet another has created a U-value calculation plugin to ArchiCAD that helps architects communicate complexity to clients with ease.

Fig 3.21 DesignLCA ArchiCAD plugin

CHANGING THE GAME

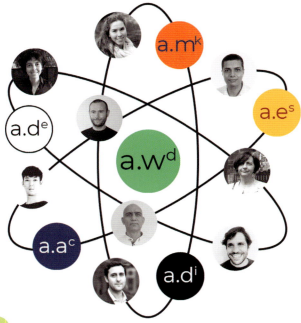

Fig 3.22 AirC World, a partnership formed by individuals to better deliver the human ecosystem

CASE STUDY

PRACTICE PROFILE: AIRC

EMBRACING TECHNOLOGY: REDEFINING OUR ROLE

Pierre Saunal is a founding partner of the small London practice, AirC Digital, which provides building information modelling (BIM) management and digital design services, alongside AirC Design, a separate company that provides architectural design services for all types of buildings. The wider practice (incorporating both companies) includes nine members of staff.

The idea of having two arms to the business was key to the founding partners, who are also architects. They identified a gap in the market associated with BIM, particularly a need within small practices requiring assistance with their workflow. The purpose here was to help small, medium and larger practices, contractors and manufacturers to embrace BIM and to utilise ArchiCAD's dynamic software. If used in the right way, it can help deliver work that large practices are delivering but at an economical rate and on a much smaller scale.

AirC also created a U-value label tool – a simple tool that highlights a fabric element skin list (i.e. brickwork, cavity, wood fibre insulation, blockwork) and attaches a U-value label to that element. This tool was created after one of the small practices they worked with requested it. Subsequently they asked Graphisoft to allow their tool to be used as a plugin for the programme.

Although not all architects may be able to code, this process shows how quickly small practitioners can see a problem, create a solution and work with the giants to implement it.

Remaining valuable in our economy demands that small practices master the art of quickly learning and implementing complicated ideas and processes. The role of the architect will continue to undergo significant change over the next 10 years due to advancements in technology, climate change concerns, urbanisation and demographic changes. New roles might include energy assessors using BIM technology, allowing us to better collaborate with MEPH engineers perhaps. Or AI tutors, allowing us to offer consultancy services to other practices.

Technology in (small) practice
To remain relevant in the marketplace, architects will have an increased reliance on technological tools such as AI, augmented reality (AR), virtual reality (VR) and other emerging technologies. AI can automate many tasks, freeing up architects to focus on more creative aspects of their work. AR and VR can enhance architects' ability to visualise designs to clients and user groups, providing more immersive experiences for them.

We will see more use of dynamic modelling platforms like cove.tool – a web-based building performance analysis and energy modeling software that optimises projects for energy, carbon and cost – empowering smaller design teams to make informed decisions. These may be more integrated with information platforms like the Greater London Authority's (GLA) webpages, which highlight local biodiversity and health equality impact. They may also be linked with sites such as UCL's 'Colouring London' platform, that defines the age, use, type and form, size, construction methodology and community groups linked to existing buildings. Indeed, we are likely to move away from single websites to more integrated platforms that pull this information together.

Technology will play a more integrated role in our adaptation. By leveraging AI and other technologies, architects can free up time to focus on learning new skills and developing their knowledge base. Online platforms and digital tools can provide architects with access to a wide range of educational resources, making it easier to keep up to date with the latest developments in their field. Furthermore, technologies like AR and VR can provide new ways for architects to visualise and communicate their designs, helping them adapt to the demands of the digital age.

As we shift to an information economy and more of the population become knowledge workers (people who solve complex problems and go beyond their field of expertise to apply them in a social, organisational and relational contexts), being a highly skilled architect becomes a key currency. As small practices, our global competitive advantage becomes not as one who *uses* these programmes (i.e. Autodesk or Graphisoft), but instead, the future will belong to those who are comfortable *building* the innovative distributed systems that run the service; for example, creating plugins for these programmes, or indeed, owning the programmes ourselves.

Adopting integrated environmental, social and economic responsive AI tools into our workflow will increase our opportunities for optimised design, helping us by providing data-driven insights and design options. AI algorithms can analyse factors such as sunlight, wind patterns, temperature and local flora to suggest the best designs or modifications, ensuring the building integrates seamlessly with the environment. Tools such as Testfit, Cove and Finch are already changing the game for small practices. By being early adopters of AI technologies, small practices may be able to distinguish themselves from competitors and provide a unique selling point to clients interested in cutting-edge design.

As a small practice, we cannot afford to be left out of our race to zero. In fact, we recognise that due to the pace of technological change and innovation, we must embrace advanced technology to improve our work/life balance, efficiency, productivity and profitability.

CHANGING THE GAME

Fig 3.23ba Generative AI image created from 'Midjourney' to help client visualise proposed design

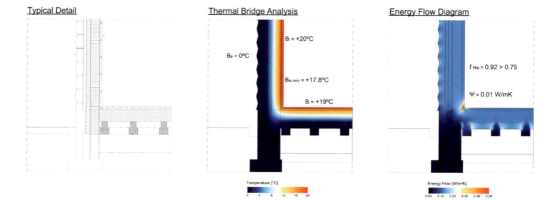

Fig 3.23b Thermal Bridging assessment within BIM authoring software (ArchiCAD) used to analyse and visualise heat loss and surface temperature at critical building junctions

Energy Performance Evaluation
N/A The Torrington

Key Values

General Project Data
Project Name:	The Torrington
City Location:	<SITE_CITY>
Latitude:	51° 41' 47" N
Longitude:	0° 9' 52" W
Altitude:	0.00 m
Climate Data Source:	Strusoft server
Evaluation Date:	22/12/2022 20:18

Building Geometry Data
Gross Floor Area:	88.78	m²
Treated Floor Area:	77.32	m²
External Envelope Area:	264.59	m²
Ventilated Volume:	223.77	m³
Glazing Ratio:	34	%

Building Shell Performance Data
Infiltration at 50Pa:	6.31	ACH

Heat Transfer Coefficients — U value [W/m²K]
Building Shell Average:	1.82
Floors:	--
External:	0.74 - 2.89
Underground:	--
Openings:	2.11 - 3.30

Specific Annual Values
Net Heating Energy:	370.38	kWh/m²a
Net Cooling Energy:	0.00	kWh/m²a
Total Net Energy:	370.38	kWh/m²a
Energy Consumption:	482.02	kWh/m²a
Fuel Consumption:	471.98	kWh/m²a
Primary Energy:	529.22	kWh/m²a
Fuel Cost:	47.20	GBP/m²a
CO₂ Emission:	101.95	kg/m²a

Degree Days
Heating (HDD):	3494.21
Cooling (CDD):	826.41

001 Existing House Thermal Block - Key Values

Geometry Data
Gross Floor Area:	88.78	m²
Treated Floor Area:	77.32	m²
Building Shell Area:	264.59	m²
Ventilated Volume:	223.77	m³
Glazing Ratio:	34	%

Internal Temperature
Min. (04:00 Feb. 09):	3.57	°C
Annual Mean:	18.05	°C
Max. (18:00 Aug. 05):	29.29	°C

Unmet Load Hours
Heating:	1153	hrs/a
Cooling:	3	hrs/a

Heat Transfer Coefficients U value [W/m²K]
Floors:	-
External:	0.74 - 2.89
Underground:	-
Openings:	2.11 - 3.30

Annual Supplies
Heating:	28636.76	kWh
Cooling:	0.00	kWh

Peak Loads
Heating (06:00 Jan. 02):	15.00	kW
Cooling (01:00 Jan. 01):	0.00	kW

Energy Consumption by Sources

Source Type	Source Name	Quantity (kWh/a)	Primary (kWh/a)	Cost (GBP/a)	CO₂ Emission (kg/a)
Renewable	Solar (Thermal & PV)	289	289	NA	0
	Wind Energy	486	486		0
Fossil	Natural Gas	36491	40140	3649	7882
	Total:	37267	40917	3649	7882

Fig 3.23c Dynamic energy modelling within BIM authoring software (ArchiCAD) used to assess energy performance of proposed buildings in 'real time' – allowing designer to iterate and gain instant feedback on energy use

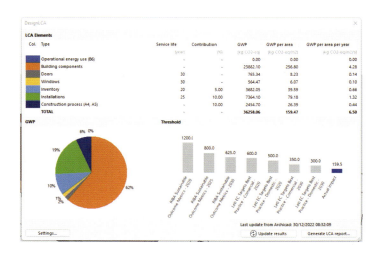

Fig 3.23d Plug-in tool (DesignLCA) within BIM authoring software (ArchiCAD) used to assess embodied carbon of proposed buildings in 'real time' – allowing designer to iterate for instant feedback on carbon intensity

It is also important to note that small practices will need to consider the implications and challenges of using AI, such as data privacy issues, the cost and time involved in learning new systems and the need for regular software updates and maintenance. It's essential to approach AI implementation with a clear understanding of both the benefits and potential difficulties.

ENVIRONMENTAL ACTIVISM

Using your voice

It is fair to say that the role of the architect is starting to shift, as it must if we are to become regenerative leaders. This shift sees architects moving towards some form of activism, pushing for a more just society.

Vanessa Nakate is a Ugandan climate activist who has gained international recognition for her efforts to bring attention to the impacts of climate change in Africa, and for her advocacy for the inclusion of African voices in global climate discussions. Nakate started her movement by holding climate strikes outside the Ugandan Parliament, emphasising the disproportionate impact of climate change from activities imposed by the Global North on the Global South, and specifically on the African continent, the second-largest continent, known for its rich biodiversity, cultural heritage, diverse ecosystems and, significantly, its low global emissions contribution. She founded the Vash Green Schools project to promote renewable energy in Ugandan schools and authored *A Bigger Picture* to share her activism journey and the urgent need for inclusive climate dialogue.[36] Her work on international platforms, including the World Economic Forum has highlighted the specific challenges Africa faces, such as severe droughts and floods. Through social media, public speaking and partnerships, Nakate is pushing for equitable global climate policies, working to ensure that the global response to climate change considers the perspectives and needs of over-extracted countries.

Small practices can lend their voices to petitions, write to MPs or join a local climate advocacy group demanding change. While we do this, we must also remember that certain types of protests are indeed a privilege and that this privilege must not be ignored; because for some, ignoring this has real-life consequences that impact safety and well-being. While a group may choose to protest as a form of activism, or indeed advocate, we must remember the intersectionalities that exclude some from certain acts of activism. For example, a Black person joining colleagues to protest on the streets in London during, say, an 'Insulate Britain campaign', carries a significantly different weight because there is a higher likelihood of that Black person being stopped, searched and arrested.[37] Even when non-ethnic minority colleagues are arrested, they have the privilege of wearing this as a badge of honour, with full confidence that, when they look for their next job, this will not reflect negatively on them. In fact, quite the opposite, it will likely be looked upon favourably. Unfortunately, at this time in the UK, no such leniency is likely to be afforded to minoritised groups. Many minoritised groups will instead experience micro-aggressions that will plague them even en route to a protest for the greater good of society; from being asked for a receipt at the till in the local shop, to being held back in a queue over others. Therefore, as we make decisions to act for the greater good, we encourage the reader to think in intersectional terms, asking themselves the question: what privileges do I have here and how can I use my privilege to create a safer space for my minoritised colleagues to fully participate in architecture and beyond? What conversations must I have the courage to broach? And how can I be an active listener and an ally to them such that I contribute to creating, ultimately, a more just society?

Fig 3.24 Vanessa Nakate, climate activist and Nobel Peace Prize nominee

Architects can learn from Nakate's influence and impact, asking ourselves questions such as how can we better use social media platforms to advance the cause of addressing our climate challenge? This determined global climate movement has emerged and we have seen more progress on the topic in the last three years than the last 30. Small practice owners cannot afford to be left out; we must lead this conversation to save the planet with the technical, creative and social tools we have at our disposal.

SOCIAL SUS
AND ENGAG

TAINABILITY
EMENT

'It is imperative that each city or community decide for itself what values it should assign to become more just.[1]
— Toni L. Griffin, Founder of urbanAC, New York

In 2023, the eighteenth International Architecture Exhibition *La Biennale di Venezia: Biennale Architettura: The Laboratory of the Future* was curated by RIBA Gold Medal 2024 winner, Professor Lesley Lokko OBE. Under the theme 'Decolonisation and Decarbonisation', Gbolade Design Studio were invited to contribute an installation sharing details of a project in Brixton, London – The LLCC. Entitled 'Regenerative Power', it examined how the building embodied a cultural, societal and physical heritage that reached far beyond its current run-down state. The Grade II-listed structure is host to two community groups: the Brixton Immortals Dominoes Club – a place of solace for older Afro-Caribbean men and their families to connect with each other – and the Brixton Soup Kitchen – a volunteer organisation serving the homeless in this part of London and beyond.

The new community centre we created placed the social and cultural ecosystems of its users at its heart; and with the Biennale exhibition we told their stories. These included the docking of the

Fig 4.1 'Regenerative Power' installation at the Venice Biennale, Gbolade Design Studio, 2023

HMT *Empire Windrush* in Tilbury on 22 June 1948, which brought workers from the West Indies to help fill post-war UK labour shortages. Dubbed the 'Windrush generation', the community faced severe intolerance and were denied access to public services and accommodation. The installation reversed this response, celebrating the rich and diverse history of the British West Indian community, and seeking to empower the West Indian community both in Brixton and far beyond.

The installation also included a 'systems' map, sprawled across one wall, physically drawing the visible and invisible connections between people, place and community. This aimed to highlight the many complex connections between these three facets, and the importance of seeking to understand them before attempting to bring about any change (i.e. the physical redevelopment of a community centre). Understanding these connections and ensuring that they remain unbroken – potentially even strengthening them – makes sure that a lasting economic, social and environmentally sustainable change may occur.

These connections between people, the buildings they inhabit (place) and the communities they engage with are what Richard Sennett refers to as the 'ambiguities' of a city.[2] They are what form the complexity of a city, which, in turn, enriches our experience of it. Our installation sought to communicate some of the salient aspects of a building project; one whose history and heritage might feed into the architectural response. Broader still, it points to the role such a project plays in the creation of local jobs – using local contractors and fabricators – as well as in improvements to health and well-being through creating spaces to 'gather' and using moss walls to filter the air. It demonstrates the strength of community already embedded, and perhaps even expanded, through the development of a building project.

Fig 4.2 Video element of the 'Regenerative Power' installation at the Venice Biennale, Gbolade Design Studio, 2023

This chapter focuses on this concept of social sustainability. We use systems thinking as a framework to address this complex concept, and stakeholder engagement as a key leverage tool to making decisions that have far-reaching consequences. We believe that in understanding the wider framework and using engagement for leverage, architects can make better decisions, grounded in an understanding of how these might influence the wider system.

SOCIAL SUSTAINABILITY

Social sustainability refers to the process of creating and maintaining equitable, healthy and liveable conditions for present and future generations. It can be described as the identification, understanding and management of the positive and negative effects that systems, processes, organisations and activities have on people and social life.[3] Social sustainability emphasises creating equitable, healthy and cohesive communities that can endure and thrive over time. It considers how present decisions affect future generations and aims to build resilience and fairness in society. It encompasses a broad array of factors, such as social equity, community engagement, cultural understanding, health and well-being, education, social cohesion, human rights and resilience. Social sustainability adopts a long-term perspective, often involving long-term planning and policy making, and considering the impact on future generations and the community's enduring vitality. It emphasises the importance of creating a society where all individuals can reach their potential, regardless of their background, identity or socio-economic status.

Social sustainability is multifaceted and is necessarily complex, therefore requiring a concerted effort across different sectors and levels of society: it cannot work without recognising the visible and invisible threads between people, places and communities – the 'stickiness' of society. To thrive in a socially sustainable neighbourhood, or city, we will require governments, organisations and individuals to work together to promote policies and practices that address the overlapping and complex interrelationships, and sometimes competing priorities, between key facets of society. For this to happen well, a clear and useful framework must be adopted.

SYSTEMS THINKING

In his book *Systems Thinking for Social Change*, consultant and author David Stroh explores how systems thinking can be applied to effectively address complex social problems.[4] Stroh emphasises the need to understand the interconnectedness of various components within a system to foster sustainable change, and introduces key principles of systems thinking – such as understanding the bigger picture, recognising patterns of behaviour and focusing on relationships rather than isolated components – to stand the best chance of addressing complexity in society.

Systems thinking provides an approach that is crucial for achieving social sustainability precisely because it focuses on the interconnectedness of issues that might at first glance seem isolated from each other. Adopting this approach will often ask of the practising architect that they observe and ask questions before attempting to respond through a design intervention. This type of thinking is precisely what a regenerative small practice must adopt and apply to respond justly in an increasingly complicated and interdependent world. When architects encounter a new project they enter into an existing social, cultural and environmental system, and a comprehensive understanding of the relationships and feedback loops within a system can lead to better decision making, reduce barriers and confrontations during design development and provide more effective interventions – even with perceived conflicting interests in projects.[5]

Several risks lay in wait when systems thinking is neglected, particularly when trying to solve complex social and environmental problems. Without a holistic view, solutions that target one area of a system can inadvertently cause issues in another. This is often referred to as 'shifting the burden', where the solution to one problem exacerbates or creates another problem elsewhere in the system.[6] A simple example of this can be the installation of internal wall insulation (IWI) in an existing terraced home in a bid to retrofit the home and contribute to decarbonising existing assets. This IWI might be installed on the front and rear facades and return on a party wall to avoid thermal bridging – as is common practice. In doing so, while reducing heat loss in the retrofitted home, the neighbouring home might become colder, requiring the neighbour to increase their gas use to heat their home, exacerbating the issue of contributing to climate change. These unintended consequences do not consider the full scope of the system (the groups of homes as part of the terrace) and often result in outcomes that can sometimes be worse than the original problem (a colder neighbouring home leading to occupier discomfort and increased use of fossil fuels), especially if they are not anticipated and managed proactively.

Another example on a larger scale relates to Southwyck House in Brixton, London. Also known as the 'Barrier Block', this Brutalist building was constructed in the 1970s on the Somerleyton Estate and spans seven storeys with 176 flats. Originally designed to shield against a never-built motorway, its inward-facing, fortress-like structure has contributed to crime by creating hidden spaces conducive to criminal activities. Its continuous facade, without windows facing the street, diminishes community interaction and natural surveillance, while the confusing layout of the complex aids criminals in escaping easily. Insufficient maintenance has led to deterioration, reinforcing neglect and fostering criminal behaviour. The building's stark aesthetics may also impact on the mental health of residents, exacerbating social withdrawal and anxiety, as is common in poorly designed homes.[7] Urban renewal efforts focusing on community integration, enhanced surveillance and improved maintenance are crucial for mitigating these issues, emphasising the need for architectural designs that consider social and psychological impacts. The architectural style and imposing nature of Southwyck House sets it apart visually and socially from the surrounding neighbourhood. This can lead to stigma and social segregation, where residents feel isolated and disconnected from the broader community. Such environments foster antisocial behaviour, both within and around the estate. The stark and imposing concrete aesthetics, coupled with the building's scale and massing, may also have a detrimental impact on mental health. Studies suggest that environments that lack natural elements – such as natural light and connection to nature – are overly harsh and feel oppressive and might contribute to anxiety and social withdrawal, conditions that may also correlate with higher crime rates.[8]

Adopting a systems thinking approach helps us to appreciate the complexity of problems that responding to the architect's brief might request of us. Ignoring this layering of challenges can lead to oversimplified solutions that do not address real issues, potentially leading to failure, frustration and distrust among local communities and governing bodies. Solutions that do not incorporate systems thinking might create dependency on certain interventions (like technological fixes or regulatory controls), which can make the system more fragile and less capable of adapting to new challenges. For architectural practices, learning from such cases highlights the importance of considering the social and psychological impacts design has on people and their well-being, thereby ensuring that our responses contribute positively to environments and support healthy, secure communities.

CASE STUDY

PROJECT PROFILE: THE LOS ANGELES ECO-VILLAGE

Now over 30 years old, the Los Angeles Eco-Village (LAEV), located in the densely populated Koreatown neighbourhood of Los Angeles, stands as a prominent model for sustainable urban living. Founded in 1993 by Lois Arkin, LAEV is a community-focused initiative that enhances environmental awareness and sustainable living within an urban setting, through design, community building and environmental stewardship in an urban village setting.

LAEV's neighbourhoods and buildings have been retrofitted to reduce energy consumption, with improvements such as high-efficiency appliances and dual-pane windows. This village has a community 'bicycle kitchen', an initiative dedicated to promoting cycling over car dependency.[9] This not only reduces carbon emissions but also fosters a sense of community among residents. Los Angeles encouragement of the use of bicycles and public transport by residents has led to a decrease in local traffic congestion and pollution.[10]

Community living is at the heart of LAEV, which operates under a co-operative governance model. This encourages resident participation in decision-making processes, ensuring that the community's operations align with the collective values of sustainability and mutual respect. The village hosts regular workshops and events focused on sustainable practices, ranging from organic gardening to waste reduction.

The integration of communal spaces, such as shared organic gardens that produce a variety of fruits and vegetables, reduces the need for packaged goods and the associated transportation emissions. Composting is another core activity, turning organic waste into valuable soil amendments for the garden. A communal kitchen and open recreational areas promote a lifestyle that values collaboration and shared responsibility. These spaces are not only functional but also serve as hubs for social interaction, reinforcing the community's tight-knit fabric. Water conservation is a critical aspect of the village's environmental strategy. The implementation of greywater systems and rainwater harvesting supplies non-potable water for irrigation and reduces the community's reliance on municipal water sources.

Arkin founded the LAEV in response to the killing of Rodney King, a Black man who had been brutally murdered by four white policemen who were acquitted. Arkin leaned into the complexity of retrofitting existing neighbourhoods to make them safe, equitable and healthy.

CHAPTER 4   SOCIAL SUSTAINABILITY AND ENGAGEMENT   **87**

Fig 4.3 LAEV playful intersection repair/intervention giving pedestrians and children priority over vehicles

    As a result, the LAEV exemplifies how sustainable design and community-oriented living can be measured, not only in environmental metrics, but also through its vibrant, supportive community. LAEV is an example of a place that does not shy away from complexity. A complexity that we will come to explore when it comes to the interrelated aspects of living.

    'Systems thinking' involves understanding how different aspects of a project (i.e. an eco-village) operate within a larger system (safety in the public realm for minoritised groups). The success of LAEV is partly due to its holistic approach to sustainability, considering environmental, social and economic factors, and asking the local community to be part of a change that was needed in a city.

To implement change within a social system, an understanding of that system is first needed. Developing a shared vision, defining success and measuring progress should come as part of best practice design development.

In local government, in commercial development corporations and even in large practices, it is common for individuals to concentrate on their specific job roles and duties, often overlooking or showing disinterest in how their work connects with others. Life appears simpler when achievable goals are set and complexity is ignored. Rarely is there a reward for understanding the entire system. Common local government adages such as 'keep it simple', 'look for quick wins' and 'pick the low-hanging fruit' embody this mindset.[11]

By contrast, Stroh utilises the ancient Indian parable of the blind men and the elephant to highlight the necessity of seeing the bigger picture.[12] In this tale, each blind man feels a different part of the elephant and believes he understands the whole animal. They are each correct in their perception of the small part of the creature they touch, but it requires their collective insights to comprehend that the elephant is the sum of all the parts they described. He further explains that when individuals only perceive fragments of a complex system, they tend to view reality through the lens of their competencies, believing they could achieve more with additional resources. This perspective often leads them to overlook the value of the contributions of others from different disciplines, and they fail to see how their actions, thoughts and intentions interact with those of other stakeholders.

Stroh employs the iceberg metaphor to differentiate between symptoms and root causes at three levels:

1. Events – the occurrences that are most visible
2. Trends and patterns – the ongoing developments over time
3. System structure – the underlying, often hidden framework that influences trends and events.

It is within the system structure (the base of the iceberg) that the greatest leverage lies for solving problems.[13] This level contains root causes shaped by numerous circular, interdependent and sometimes time-delayed relationships among its components. Elements such as policies or final design proposals may be readily observable, whereas others, like perceptions and purposes, are less apparent.

This deeper level of understanding is crucial yet frequently overlooked in our efforts to address problems quickly and simply. Yet, it demands genuine expertise, willingness to take risks and a commitment to enduring the time it takes to implement solutions. Stroh outlines a 'four-stage change process' that elicits change articulating the discrepancy between current realities and desired aspirations.

1. Establishing a change-ready foundation: this might be establishing a shared vision
2. Defining and accepting responsibility for the current realities at all iceberg levels
3. Making a deliberate decision to pursue the stated aspirations
4. Initiating actions to close the gap through strategic interventions, broadening stakeholder engagement and learning from experiences.

While we can choose any of the above key points to expand upon, we believe the most important stage for this section of the book is to look at the actions that might have the largest leverage – that is, the 'what is unseen'. These are the system structures responsible for a particular pattern of behaviour – say the increase in crime on an estate as in the example of Southwyck House, or the negative implications for the mental health of people in poorly designed homes.[14] As small business practitioners, we are usually more directly able to be in control of, or indeed advocate for, broadening stakeholder engagement as part of our design and development process due to the structure of our client-project relationships. These are usually closer and more direct than with larger teams with a range of design, project management and economic assessment consultants. Small practices are inherently more flexible in our ability to identify and approach stakeholders without bureaucracy. The closeness small practices build with clients allows for deeper relationships. As small practices tend to work on local projects and are inherently more embedded within communities, they have opportunities to leverage this local presence to engage directly with community members and local stakeholders. This facilitates more effective and meaningful dialogues that respect and integrate local insights and needs.

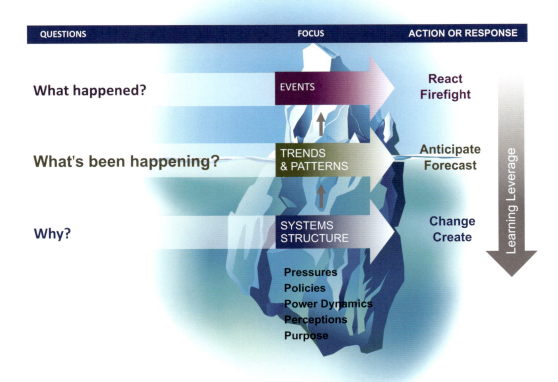

Fig 4.4 The iceberg metaphor as used by David Stroh in *Systems Thinking for Social Change*

CASE STUDY

PROJECT PROFILE:
DAGENHAM HEATHWAY BY URBAN SYMBIOTICS

Fig 4.5 Stakeholder engagement and Dagenham Heathway shop, Urban Symbiotics

CHAPTER 4   SOCIAL SUSTAINABILITY AND ENGAGEMENT

Urban Symbiotics was founded by architect Stephanie Edwards and product designer James Stewart as a practice focused on people-centric urban planning and community engagement. They concentrate on creating masterplans and high-street strategies, while involving the community in the decision-making process. Community engagement is seen as a primary tool and a means to foster innovation.

Over time, Edwards and Stewart have developed skills beyond masterplanning and they now count 'participatory design' as a key specialism, and one they are becoming well known for. They are mainly employed by local authorities and large developers to work with community groups to identify needs and wants, fears and constraints to design. They offer this as a stand-alone service, or as part of a wider scope that may or may not include masterplanning.

A key area of concern in participatory design is gaining the trust of the community – this is particularly important in cases where trust in design and planning may has been diminished by past disappointments and led to scepticism within the community.

Urban Symbiotics use various strategies to facilitate this process – including setting up pop-up shops in community centres – to allow the team to interact with the local community directly. They held one such pop-up at the Dagenham Heathway Station when working on engagement for Be First, the delivery arm of Barking and Dagenham Council. Pop-ups like these enable them to understand local demographics, as well as providing an opportunity for stakeholder mapping and identifying community influencers who can help develop 'trust routes' as part of the engagement process.

THE TIMELINE

LISTEN & UNDERSTAND

The first stage in the timeline is where the team embed themselves in the community to engage in conversation with residents. We listen and record the insights from every conversation, helping us understand the unique concerns, hopes, and ideas related to the Heathway. So far, we've run a pop-up outside the station, a stall at the shopping centre Christmas fair, and ideas wall at the library and continue to strike up conversations with local businesses and from our newly open shop. (drop-in on a Thursday for a chat!!)

CREATE TOGETHER

So once we've captured all the concerns, hopes and ideas for the Heathway, we will analyse them and produce a list of "My Heathway Themes." These may be the identity of the Heathway, shopping on the Heathway, activities for young people etc. We will then ask the community to participate in focus groups where we can turn themes into workable concepts that can provide the foundation for the community vision.

CELEBRATE & SHARE

The final stage will be to share the vision that we developed together with the local neighbourhood and get final community backing before finalising the document. We're hoping that this will take the form of a celebration on the Heathway where all those involved can celebrate their ideas and share the vision with their friends and family.

Jan 22   Feb 22   Mar 22   Apr 22   May 22   Jun 22   Jul 22   Aug 22   Sep 22   Oct 22   Nov 22   Dec 22   Jan 23   Feb 23   Mar 23   Apr 23   May 23

Fig 4.6   Dagenham and Heathway community engagement programme, Urban Symbiotics

The Urban Symbiotics team make a point of meeting people where they are: churches, community centres, care homes. In the case of Dagenham Heathway they set up an engagement stall right outside Barking and Dagenham Tube station, making themselves visible and accessible.
As part of their works, they prepared a website to keep residents and interested parties informed about the works at Dagenham Heathway.

Urban Symbiotics' ethos is that when the community feels listened to, it creates a powerful force for change. Moreover, these engagement processes can give rise to local innovation – unique solutions that address the specific needs and challenges of a community. From redesigning a high street to rethinking how a housing estate is retrofitted, these projects show that sustainable, community-driven design is not only possible but also hugely beneficial.

Fig 4.7 Stakeholder engagement: Becontree Design Code idea boards, Urban Symbiotics

Fig 4.8 'Be First' Dagenham and Heathway Community Shop opening; designed to collect ideas, Urban Symbiotics

> **Innovation:** Small practices often exhibit higher levels of innovation and creativity due to fewer bureaucratic barriers. They can experiment with new ideas and technologies and promote sustainable building methods, materials and designs. This can be particularly appealing to stakeholders looking for unique, customised solutions rather than standard, off-the-shelf designs.
>
> **Resource management:** Given their size, small practices often need to operate within tighter constraints than larger firms. This can lead to more thoughtful resource management, a key aspect of social sustainability. In small practices, the principals or lead architects often take a hands-on approach to projects, engaging directly with stakeholders. This direct involvement can reassure stakeholders that their input is directly influencing the project outcome, enhancing trust and engagement.
>
> **Value-driven practice:** Small practices often choose projects that align with their values, which can include social sustainability. They can therefore advocate for socially sustainable outcomes even in the face of opposition or apathy.

Starting projects with a shared vision can often go a long way to determining success when it comes to social sustainability and social value. In his book *Systems Architypes*, Daniel Kim suggests we find ways to make teams (a broad term, encompassing groups such as occupants of a building) collaborators rather than competitors.[15] Depending on the complexity of a project, failing to identify this shared vision as part of a social sustainability approach will inevitably lead to delivery risks, such as resistance from a vocal community group. In addressing social sustainability, practices can foresee and mitigate the potential social risks of a project. A major risk many face today is the push-back from community groups when they do not believe a development is in keeping with their local community aspirations. This is seen in the many applications that get rejected with the listed reasons for rejection ranging from 'detrimental impact on neighbouring amenity' through to 'negative effect on character and appearance'.[16] By engaging with these communities from the outset, projects can save on costly setbacks and reputational damage in the future.

As evidenced by Urban Symbiotics, small practices are often uniquely placed for designing and delivering socially sustainable projects. Some might bring local knowledge, as they are often deeply embedded in their local communities, possessing a strong understanding of local conditions, culture and needs. This can allow them to reach the point of 'trust' with local communities much easier than larger practices might, as well as being able to offer design solutions that are socially and culturally appropriate, fostering social cohesion and inclusion.

A JUST CITY

We strongly believe that creating a regenerative practice will require us to think differently, behave differently and, ultimately, act differently. In *It's Not That Radical*, Mikaela Loach redefines the discourse on climate change, asserting that the solution lies in racial equality and a means to build a better world for all, without regard to class, colour, location or any other factor that currently defines an individual.[17] She emphasises that the climate crisis originates from the very systems of oppression that continue to harm people today. Addressing social inequity in architecture is a complex issue that involves considering not only the physical designs of our buildings and cities, but also how these designs impact and interact with various aspects of people's lives. In doing so, we must be cognisant of who we invite to the decision-making table.

Adopting an engagement approach that is more equitable is part of a 'just transition', which ensures that the shift towards a more sustainable and regenerative future is fair and equitable for all individuals and communities involved.[18] It recognises that transitioning to a more sustainable and regenerative society will have social and economic implications, and aims to address and mitigate any potential negative impacts on marginalised groups or workers in industries that may be affected by the transition.

A just transition involves several key principles including social equity, worker rights and protection, environmental justice, and community engagement and participation. This last point on participation is emphasised by Ayana Elizabeth Johnson in her book *All We Can Save*, where she stresses the importance of involving communities that may be impacted in the decision-making processes, ensuring their voices are heard.[19] Specifically, she underlines the importance of including a wide range of voices, particularly women's voices, in the climate conversation. She argues that diverse perspectives lead to more innovative and comprehensive solutions to the climate crisis. Moreover, she highlights that women, who are often disproportionately impacted by climate change – for example, with women in Europe earning 13% less per hour than men, single women are more likely to have difficulties paying their energy bills than single men[20] – play a critical role in the climate movement and are also at the forefront of innovative solutions and leadership.[21]

In understanding how a just transition might occur, it is worth considering what a just city might look like. Here, we can turn to Toni Griffin, planner and professor at Harvard Graduate School. In her work, 'Defining the Just City Beyond Black and White', Griffin sets out her 10 key principles for what a just city might look like. She emphasises that these principles cannot be decreed from above but should emerge from the values that each community deems important.[22] The aim is to foster clear intentions and a collectively developed definition of justice so that when a city achieves an ideal state, its characteristics are recognisable and celebrated.

The values listed below therefore serve as an initial approach to guide the design process and are aimed at fostering equitable and inclusive urban environments:

1. Equity: Ensuring the fair distribution of both material and non-material resources to maximise the benefit to any given community.

2. Choice: Providing communities with a range of options concerning places, programme, amenities and decisions to enhance their agency.

3. Access: Facilitating easy proximity or connection to essential services, quality amenities and opportunities.

4. Connectivity: Establishing networks, both social and spatial, that link people and places, thus enabling access and opportunities for all.

5. Ownership: Empowering individuals and communities to have a stake in processes, outcomes or physical assets.

6. Diversity: Embracing varied programme, peoples and cultural norms within the built environment and in decision-making processes.

> **7. Participation:** Ensuring diverse voices are heard and actively involved in issues impacting their social and spatial well-being.
>
> **8. Inclusion and belonging:** Promoting an environment that accepts differences, integrates diverse perspectives and ensures spaces are integrative and safe.
>
> **9. Beauty:** Upholding everyone's right to well-crafted and thoughtfully designed surroundings.
>
> **10. Creative innovation:** Encouraging creativity in problem-solving and in developing interventions that enhance the quality of place.

A just transition acknowledges that the transition to a more sustainable, indeed a more just society, should not come at the expense of vulnerable communities or workers, but rather should provide opportunities for a more equitable and prosperous future for all. In this way, participation is therefore key.

ADOPTING A PARTICIPATORY DESIGN PROCESS

A participatory design process that encourages community involvement can ensure that a wider range of voices and perspectives are heard. This process can lead to more equitable solutions that meet the specific needs of the community – both in short-term social value outcomes, and longer-term social sustainability impacts. The RIBA have developed the Social Value Toolkit to help architects deliver social value in their work. The toolkit provides a step-by-step process for embedding social value from the outset of a project.[23] It highlights the key dimensions of social value, including jobs and apprenticeships, well-being generated by design, designing with the community, learning developed through construction and constructing buildings using local materials.[24] Importantly, this toolkit includes a series of social value, post-occupancy evaluation questions, such as, 'do you think your neighbourhood is a good place to live?', as well as questions surrounding the emotions people feel about their neighbourhoods and those about connectedness to neighbours and nature. Questions around freedom and flexibility that probe feelings of safety and privacy are also included alongside questions around participation, where respondents can speak about how much they felt a part of the redesign process.[25]

Robust stakeholder engagement processes and systems have started to be developed and are becoming more widely understood in our industry. Stakeholder engagement in its current form has been born out of the public outcry for more local involvement in the shaping of places, neighbourhoods, towns and cities. While companies like Social Life have always had a role in this space, more and more interdisciplinary practices are springing up to meet this rising need.[26] By involving community members in the design- and decision-making processes, architects can create spaces that truly reflect the needs, values and aspirations of the people they serve.

The process of thorough and in-depth stakeholder engagement is one many small practices are starting to undertake. It is important to note that this requires its own scope of service and should be viewed (and charged) as such. A more complex project, such as an infrastructure masterplan, will likely require more nuanced community engagement processes, and small businesses may be unable to accommodate this service with current staffing numbers. Therefore care must be taken when choosing what level of involvement a small or medium-sized practice can have, and it is worth considering partnering with another practice, with one leading on 'architecture' and the other on 'engagement'. From a business perspective, it could even present an opportunity to branch out beyond your usual services and develop the knowledge to include an additional service to your practice.

A framework for participatory design: stakeholder engagement
1. Stakeholder mapping: clearly identifying stakeholders and community representatives
It's vital to understand the demographic composition, interest groups, local authorities and other key stakeholders in a project. Engage with community leaders who can provide insights and connections within the community.

Using the leverage of local partners and collaborators takes advantage of existing 'trust routes', which can be built on to maximise the impact of engagement. Collaborating with local organisations, schools or businesses to tap into existing community networks and utilise local knowledge and expertise ensures that engagement activities are culturally sensitive and relevant.

It is important to seek out voices that may often be excluded from these discussions. With community engagement, we often find that some voices are louder than others, or indeed, some demographics. For example, older retirees may have more time to engage than younger people and therefore, young people are often excluded in the making and managing of their neighbourhoods.

An example worth expanding on is a toolkit that includes young people in the engagement process: the free youth engagement toolkit 'Voice, Opportunity, Power', developed by ZCD Architects, Grosvenor, TCPA and Sports England. The toolkit aims to empower young people to actively participate in community development, particularly in urban redevelopment projects.[27] It encourages young people to voice their opinions, offers them opportunities to influence decisions and equips

Fig 4.9   Student engagement 'block playing' workshop

them with the power to implement their ideas. Key takeaways include practical engagement strategies for involving young people in shaping their neighbourhoods and ensuring they have significant input in the future developments of their communities. This approach not only involves discussions and the development of ideas, but also compensates young participants for their contributions.

> The toolkit comprises 5 sessions:
>
> **Session 1** focuses on lived experience including teaching new mapping and analysis skills.
>
> **Session 2** asks participants to 'show their neighbourhoods' with an aim of analysing the local neighbourhood using a traffic-light system.
>
> **Session 3** encourages participants to ask for what they might want to see in a new development, including briefing the design team.
>
> **Session 4** empowers participants by asking for feedback on development designs based on earlier discussions.
>
> **Session 5** is an opportunity for the design team to demonstrate how they have responded to the ideas of the participants, where design and development proposals can be challenged or endorsed.

2. Develop a comprehensive engagement strategy

It is important that clear objectives, timelines and methods for engagement are outlined. This is a detailed piece of work and should not be taken lightly. Building in flexibility ensures that the strategy can be adapted based on feedback and changing needs. In developing a strategy, we must ensure inclusivity. This requires making efforts to include marginalised and under-represented groups, considering factors such as the time and location of a meeting to accommodate different schedules and accessibility needs. Use inclusive language and facilitation methods that encourage participation from all attendees.

An example of this is the Mayor of London's 'Good Growth by Design' programme. This includes the research and engagement paper 'Safety in Public Space: Women, Girls and Gender Diverse People', which focuses on women's safety in public spaces and the importance of gender-inclusive urban development.[28] It emphasises the need for comprehensive policies and strategies, community involvement and inclusive programming to ensure women's safety, and expands on the concept of safety in public spaces being multifaceted and extending beyond merely avoiding crime. The paper advocates that safety can be comprehended through three lenses: freedom from violence, harassment and intimidation; usability of spaces; and a sense of belonging. These elements significantly affect the experiences and behaviours of women, girls and gender-diverse individuals in public settings, influencing how these spaces are designed and utilised.

Implicit safety concerns are central to understanding these experiences. Women often ask themselves if they feel free from the threat of violence and engage in 'safety work', which includes altering their routes, being vigilant about their surroundings and using objects like keys for self-defence to mitigate feelings of vulnerability. Moreover, societal conditioning plays a role in how safety is perceived. From a young age, girls learn to navigate public spaces with caution due to the threat of male aggression. Surveys in London reveal that a substantial majority of women frequently feel unsafe (a figure higher among women aged 18–24), especially on public transport and after dark, affecting their willingness to venture out.[29]

Violence and harassment in public spaces are alarmingly common, with a significant proportion of women experiencing sexual harassment or more severe threats. These risks are even higher for women of colour, disabled women and LGBTQIA+ individuals, who face compounded threats due to intersectional discrimination. Despite the prevalence of compound experiences of sexism – including racism, transphobia, ableism, homophobia and LGBTQIA+ discrimination, classism and ageism – support services for gender-diverse individuals remain inadequate, highlighting a critical area of concern in public safety and urban planning.

Key takeaways from the 'Safety in Public Space' document include the importance of a 24-hour strategy and local action plan, community programming and management, transparent communication and engagement with the community. The document also highlights case studies and initiatives that have addressed women's safety and provides recommended resources for further reading. It calls for action and experimentation in creating gender-inclusive public spaces, challenging traditional approaches, and prioritising the needs and experiences of women, girls and gender-diverse people.[30]

Fig 4.10 Buller's Girls' School site visit to Viella Land construction site

There are 10 key questions that can be asked during design stages, as highlighted in the 'Safety for Women' report:

Project set-up
1. Is project leadership addressing exclusion?
2. Is the project team gender informed and diverse?
3. Is the project budget appropriate?

Understanding
4. Are you practising inclusive engagement?
5. Is your data collection process adopting inclusivity principles?

Making
6. Are you adopting genuine co-design with women, girls and gender-diverse people?
7. Are your design features gender-informed?
8. Are you considering diversity and inclusion issues beyond the site boundary?

Using
9. Are appropriate policies and strategies in place to support women's safety in the longer term?
10. Is there an agreed approach to continuing community programming in the space?[31]

3. Utilise various communication channels
Using diverse methods of communication, including public meetings, workshops, social media and surveys (in-person and online), to reach different segments of the community remains key to sharing knowledge and harnessing information far and wide. Facilitate workshops and public meetings where community members can express their views, ask questions and collaborate on ideas. Use interactive tools and exercises to engage participants actively, such as design charrettes,

Fig 4.11 Brixton Soup Kitchen barbeque. An example of approachable engagement as a way to break down barriers for vulnerable people, allowing them to ask for help

Fig 4.12 The Dominoes Club. The architecture project design team played dominoes with the host, building a relationship and fostering trust

focus groups or participatory mapping. Use digital platforms for virtual meetings, online surveys such as Commonplace, or interactive tools, ensuring that technology enhances rather than hinders participation.[32] It is just as important to create a suite of accessible and understandable materials that cater to various literacy levels and languages spoken within a particular community. From sketches to foam models, pin-ups to radio stations, the opportunities to reach people where they are remains key.

The RIBA have created the 'Engagement Overlay' to the RIBA Plan of Work. This is a framework designed to enhance stakeholder engagement throughout all stages of building projects. Developed in collaboration with the Association of Collaborative Design (ACD) and Sustrans, and supported by the Landscape Institute, this overlay provides architects and other built-environment professionals with guidance on how to effectively engage with communities and stakeholders. Its main goal is to standardise engagement processes to ensure inclusivity and transparency, thereby improving project outcomes and contributing to the creation of healthier and more adaptable communities.

The RIBA Engagement Overlay emphasises the importance of early and proportionate engagement, facilitating stakeholder participation from the initial stages of a project through to its planning and execution. By doing so, it helps to reduce the risks surrounding projects by mitigating potential conflicts and challenges through collaborative decision-making processes. Additionally, the Overlay serves as a resource for built-environment professionals to better understand and implement high-quality engagement processes, which are increasingly required in procurement frameworks and social value assessments.

Overall, the RIBA Engagement Overlay aims to elevate engagement standards across the industry, fostering accountability and enhancing the environments where people live, work and socialise.

Fig 4.13 Grahame Park community engagement workshop using gingerbread models to engage with the public for feedback

4. Create continuous feedback loops
Establish regular channels for communication and feedback throughout the project's lifecycle. This was the strategy Urban Symbiotics used in the development of the Purley High Street development framework for Croydon Council. The final output for this piece of work included the more traditional framework document for Croydon Council, but alongside this was a website to keep the community informed of progress, challenges and changes, and that seeks continuous input.

5. Demonstrate transparency and integrity
It is important to be open about a project's scope, limitations and decision-making processes so as not to give false hope, or damage hard-won relationships by inadvertently contributing to mistrust between community groups and organisations like the local authority or indeed developers. Community members have valid concerns and criticisms that must be acknowledged and addressed in a respectful and transparent manner. Therefore, it is often good practice to identify and highlight from the outset exactly how much influence a community group, or local residents, can have on the evolution of a proposal.

Fig 4.14 Grahame Park community engagement workshop with design development proposals and models shared with the public for feedback

6. Evaluate and reflect

Assess the effectiveness of community engagement activities and make necessary adjustments in real time by reflecting on the insights gained and how they have shaped the project, ensuring that community input is genuinely integrated into the design. A key metric could be, if long-term relationships were built, the maintaining of such relationships beyond the project's completion and ongoing collaboration.

Done well, social value should incorporate engagement from a wide variety of stakeholders. It should be able to point to some clear outcomes, including evidence of local job creation and economic growth; opportunities for increased feelings of health and well-being; positive environmental impacts; and the demonstration of a strength of community.[33]

As the guardians of the built environment, architects are entrusted with an immense responsibility. This is not merely to design beautiful, functional structures, but to craft spaces that foster community, promote social well-being and stand as beacons of inclusivity. As the world grapples with rapid urbanisation, climate challenges and social disparities, the regenerative architect community must rise to the occasion, leading the charge in integrating social sustainability into every facet of our work. This is not just a moral imperative but a foundational aspect of building a resilient, harmonious future for all.

CASE STUDY

PRACTICE PROFILE: STUDIO GIL

Studio Gil is a London-based architecture and design practice established in 2009. They blend design sensibility and craft with social agency, working closely with ethnic minority groups and organisations, listening to the often-unheard voices of marginalised communities, translating their stories into architectural propositions.

As part of their designs for the Wolves Lane Centre, Studio Gil have developed a masterplan for the Market Garden City site in Wood Green, north London. The project revitalises a dilapidated site, retaining glasshouses and adding community assets, such as teaching and learning spaces. The design emphasises circular economy principles – using carbon-sequestering materials – and will host diverse activities, representing the cultural heritage of the local community. The Wolves Lane Centre will be an ecological flagship for food growing and community interaction.

Critically, the design and construction phases are seen as crucial moments for educational and collaborative opportunities, empowering the local community by shifting expertise and decision-making from professionals to the site's users. As a result, the design of the project places a significant focus on circular economy principles, utilising a range of natural materials that capture carbon instead of releasing it. These materials are chosen for their ease of maintenance and adaptability. This approach will transform the Wolves Lane Centre into a leading model for ecological food production and community engagement in Wood Green.

Fig 4.15 Wolves Lane engagement session; director Pedro Gil shares design development proposals

ECONO
SUSTAIN

MIC ABILITY

'You never change things by fighting the existing reality. To change something, build a new model that makes the existing model obsolete.'
— Buckminster Fuller, Architect

THE POWER OF SMALL

When looking at changing the game of architectural design practice, from an economic sustainability standpoint the opportunities are enormous. On a global level, small and medium-sized enterprises (SMEs) have a critical role to play through their contribution to the health of the national economy and employment. Staggeringly, SMEs make up 90% of businesses globally, creating two out of every three jobs worldwide. They also support the livelihoods of over two billion people and are fundamental to global supply chains operating smoothly.[1]

According to the UK Department for Business, Energy and Industrial Strategy (BEIS), 99.9% of the 5.51 million businesses in the UK are small: defined as those employing no more than 49 people. 36,900 businesses employ up to 249 employees and make up the remaining contribution to the SME-sized businesses. Nearly a fifth of all these businesses operate in the construction sector, with 883,000 such companies employing 1.835 million people.[2]

SMEs are evidently key to the economic strength of most countries, in both less- and more-economically developed environments. They can:

- **Adjust rapidly to change:** decisions can be taken by managers and implemented throughout the company expediently.

- **Pivot quickly** to new and developing markets: analysing areas for growth and quickly targeting new opportunities.

- **Adopt innovative working practices and use of technology:** the cost of training is reduced due to smaller numbers of staff, so new technology or working methods can be applied on projects and schemes far more quickly.

- **Create agile working environments and allow flexible working hours:** SMEs are often employee-focused; a major benefit for those who cannot fit the 9am to 5pm working day.

- **Benefit from quick and greater buy-in:** with staff members adopting company visions and goals through a one-team ethos.[3]

In an increasingly complex, competitive and fluctuating commercial environment, the sustained adoption and integration of holistic sustainability principles might be daunting for most SMEs. However, it is crucial for SME organisations to have steady and sustainable growth, and we posit that their/our/your economic survival increasingly depends on it.[4] Furthermore, to address what SME businesses might need to do to be sustainable in their operating spheres, we suggest that the current economic models of SME business growth and development need to be challenged and reframed.

From a business perspective, architects sit within the sphere of professional services – people with a specialist knowledge whom others engage for their services. Other professional services providers include dentists, doctors, management consultants, lawyers and accountants, to name but a few. An interesting observation we've made regarding this group, is that professional services providers often come to accept long-standing modes of operation; they are rarely quick at innovating, or at adopting radical methods of capturing, recycling and sharing the knowledge they possess. This might be, in part, due to a fear of losing their 'gatekeeper' status; or it may be a result of multifarious regulatory, legislative, administrative and training requirements, that consume so many practices, and which result in the status quo being maintained.[5]

There needs to be a paradigm shift in how professions, and especially SME architects, model their businesses. The need for a resilient, dynamic and forward-thinking approach to practice management is essential today, especially considering the turbo-charged technological advances in virtual reality, automation, artificial intelligence and more.

RE-DEFINING ECONOMICS AND ECONOMIC SUSTAINABILITY

Our world, whether we like it not, is ruled by economics. Taking a quick detour back to ancient Greek times, the definition of economics originates from the words *oikos*, meaning 'household', and *nomos*, meaning 'rules' or 'norms'. This essentially translates to 'household management', coined by the philosopher Xenophon (b.431 bc) in his Socratic dialogue, *Oeconomicus*. Many others have since attempted to define economics, and a widely accepted contemporary definition is given by Gregory Mankiw, author of *Principles of Economics*, who suggested that, 'Economics is the study of how society manages its scare resources.'[6]

To become truly sustainable, we need to reconsider the economic arguments for sustainable development: why should people who desire more sustainable homes/products/cars be penalised more than those who don't? How is it sensible or responsible that doing more good costs more? Why does society and the economic models of global business make it more profitable to exploit resources, land and people, leaving destruction in their wake for generations to come?

As well as addressing the ways small practices can deliver more economically sustainable projects through practice, we also propose creative ways to operate and manage more sustainable businesses for the long term.

So, what do we mean by economic sustainability? The term can be readily defined as business/commercial/organisational practices that support the long-term economic development of a company or nation, while also protecting environmental, social and cultural elements.[7]

Fig 5.1 Economics; an illustrative definition

Over the last three quarters of a century, probably since shortly after the Second World War, the success, progress and productivity of national economies has largely focused on one metric: gross domestic product (GDP). Yet, when considered alongside global sociopolitical events and the current climate crisis, the appropriateness of rising GDP as a true definition of success has been brought into question.

It is now becoming very apparent that universal acceptance of GDP as a positive indicator to support national-scale development has only served to promote unsustainable business practices, inequalities in wealth and health resource allocation, and exploitation. Humans have collectively created a global civilisation that is primarily shaped by a system that pays little or no regard to the fundamental processes that maintain the healthy function of ecological systems.

Conventional economics, and crucially, economic theory espoused in academic institutions, seems to justify the over-exploitation of resources in the short term for self-interested individual human consumption, without regard to the long-term impact on vital ecosystem functions, upon which all life depends. Contemporary economics presents arguments for the replacement of diversity with business systems of a single mindset, which structurally embed competition and maximum resource use. In natural (non-man-made) ecosystems, this approach actively drives the weakening of natural resilience, which depends on redundancies at multiple scales. In society today, the use of the word 'redundant' or 'redundancy' implies something unnecessary, of little use or purpose, and readily discarded. However, in living systems, having redundancies across various functions is crucial for maintaining life in the most natural and organic way.[8] For example, in the natural world, ecosystemic redundancy implies that the loss of a species is compensated by other species that contribute a similar function; thereby providing a degree of resilience to the whole ecosystem. Learning from natural ecological systems, it is much harder to disrupt vital functions if they are distributed or decentralised (i.e. performed simultaneously at multiple scales and locations), rather than if these functions are performed at one large, centralised location, which is geographically efficient but lacking in resilience and flexibility.

Ecology describes the natural function, relationships and evolution of living systems within an ecosystem. The dynamics that control global, national and local ecological systems shouldn't really be open for political discussion. Unfortunately, however, humans have made this the case. Societies are increasingly recognising their mistake in allowing this to happen. They concede that current 'big business' commercial activities need to pivot away from purely capitalistic, resource-exploitative and revenue-focused models towards regenerative operational modes in order to stem and reverse the resulting climatic impact. Rather than promoting continuous growth economics, we need to push for a circular, cooperative, regenerative and distributive value system. Emerging economic theorists exploring how to radically transition global economic thinking through links to nature and ecology include Nate Hagens, creator of *The Great Simplification* podcast, and Kate Raworth, author of *Doughnut Economics*.[9]

Businesses have rarely been obligated to pay for the toll their operations take on the world. The social and environmental costs are largely hidden from their accounting statements. However, the economic impact of rising transportation costs, wages, fuel, energy and materials are directly and immediately impactful enough on profitability to make business leaders sit up and take note.

It has been observed that it is 'generally cheaper for consumers to buy a product that has a worse impact on its environment than the equivalent product that does less harm'.[10] This is largely because environmental costs are secondary to monetary costs at every level of business. If we measure the environmental cost of a product, and apportion its financial value accordingly, the reverse becomes true. However, if we're thinking regeneratively, we need to go further than this.

A product should do more good rather than just doing less harm. The fashion industry provides an apt and oft-cited example. This is an industry that is extremely notorious for being carbon-resource intensive, producing high levels of pollution and encouraging so-called 'fast-fashion' consumption.

But let's imagine a scenario where these hidden expenses could be accurately measured and allocated. Consider reaching a stage where the most affordable t-shirt also happened to have the least detrimental (or even positive) impact on the environment and society. In this situation, consumers seeking bargains would harmonize seamlessly with business strategies that promote a balanced and equitable planet. This alignment would harness the potent influence of market dynamics to advance the objectives of sustainability and achieve the ultimate economic goal of 'true cost accounting'.[11] What if we could make it more economically beneficial for businesses to reduce their environmental impact, therefore allowing consumers to base their decision-making on this form of accounting or what we might call the 'whole life cost' to the built environment?

An exploitative method of product design and delivery is commonplace in all industries. The time is now (some could argue it has passed) for businesses to stop relying on the capitalistic thirst we've developed for exponential financial growth and the ensuing harmful environmental practices required to maintain that.

We're confident that most of you reading this book are already taking steps to shape your organisations, businesses and projects to make a positive difference in your sphere of influence within the built environment. What we really hope is that this book will inspire you further by reframing the lens through which the largely fiscal element of sustainability is viewed.

SUSTAINABLE ECONOMICS IN ACTION

A global mindset shift is required to radically rethink business models fit for a regenerative future. Small organisations can and must play their part just as much as the big conglomerates. There are examples of both small to medium-sized businesses and a number of large organisations from other industries that are making, or have already undertaken, the transition towards more sustainable business practices. Assuming you are a leader, or employee, within a SME organisation, it is possible to learn from larger companies by taking a lateral thinking perspective. Ask yourself: how could we apply this at our significantly smaller scale? What are the golden nuggets of insight from this large, multi-thousand employee corporation that we could adopt within our four-person business? Could we implement their approach while using our scale and nimbleness to operate more regeneratively across our social, economic and environmental footprints?

Visit *The Great Simplification* podcast website

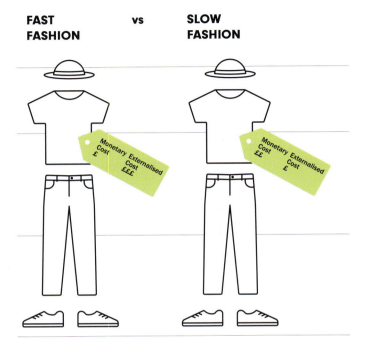

Fig 5.2 The relative costs of fast and slow fashion showing the cost of the product against the associated environmental cost of production

Fast fashion – low cost, low quality, unsustainable	Slow fashion – higher quality, more expensive, more sustainable
Typically consumes significant volumes of water, e.g. 700 gallons per cotton shirt, 2,000 gallons per pair of jeans	Uses recycled and upcycled materials, such as fabrics made from second-hand clothing
Uses microplastics such as polyester, nylon and acrylics, which typically take hundreds of years to biodegrade	Sustainable materials that are naturally biodegradable and bio-based, such as wool, wild silk, organic cotton, linen, hemp and lyocell
Manufacturers often need to over-work factories and low-paid staff to make production facilities economically viable, leading to poor working conditions	Retailers invest in raising re-use/recycle/repair approach among consumers by providing these services
High volumes of products created require energy-intense processes	Manufacturers source materials from ethical producers, both environmentally and socially
Waste from textile production disposed into natural ecosystems and watercourses	Retailers reduce/omit packaging at the point of sale

Table 5.1 Fast versus slow fashion, the impact trade-off. Adapted from Yvon Chouinard, Jib Ellison and Rick Ridgeway, 'The Sustainable Economy', *Harvard Business Review*

RE-EVALUATING AND REVALUING

We can't talk about cost in the built environment without talking about embodied carbon. Thankfully, this is something that is increasingly recognised as a key measure in the performance and suitability of a construction material. Embodied carbon represents the emissions associated with the production of a material and its use in construction throughout the whole lifecycle of a building or infrastructure project. Below are some measures of embodied carbon of commonly used construction materials for the casing surrounding air source heat pumps (ASHPs), as researched for a typical UK residential housing project:

Design variation	Embodied carbon (kg CO_2e/m^2)
Cross laminated timber ASHP	409
Steel frame ASHP	759
Concrete frame ASHP	517
Timber frame ASHP	423

Table 5.2 Embodied carbon figures of typical construction project with common building materials, source: Environmental Audit Committee, UK Parliament[14]

Of the three main superstructure materials used in the construction of buildings, steel is by far the most carbon intensive during manufacture. Concrete usually has the largest embodied carbon measure in any given project, although this is not down to the material itself, but rather due to our over-dependence and wide-scale use of it as a substructure and superstructure material. When compared with other materials, it has a comparatively low carbon footprint and is typically less expensive to produce as its raw materials can be sourced locally in most cases. Furthermore, it has circular economy benefits as it can be created using industrial by-products such as wood ash and cement kiln dust. Concrete can also be recycled once a building has been demolished. The key point to communicate across the industry is that rather than eliminating its use, there is a need to significantly reduce our over-reliance on concrete as a structural system when other materials, such as timber, are inherently regenerative and can provide the same structural function in hybrid forms. Similarly, recycled steel reduces the embodied carbon associated with production by up to two-thirds when compared with its virgin counterpart. Timber stands out as the most carbon efficient of the three due to its carbon sequestering ability, but it does have its limitations for larger and taller buildings and infrastructure, where concrete and steel have undoubtable benefits.

The industry is increasingly aware of the need to re-use and recycle concrete and steel components, as well as increased application of timber structures. There is also a growing development of non-structural circular and bio-based materials that make up the fabric, finishes and interiors of buildings, and can help significantly reduced their whole-lifecycle carbon costs. Such materials include bio-based paints and coatings, wood wool board, clay plasterboard, wood-fibre insulation, cork wall linings and hemp insulation.

CASE STUDY

BUSINESS PROFILE: WHITE STAMP

White Stamp are an architect-led Portuguese start-up/SME operating in the fashion sector, and breaking ground with its circular clothing market proposition. Their simple but effective concept is to connect the first- and second-hand clothes markets through a circular consumption model. Their intention is to scale this right across the fashion industry by partnering with larger clothing brands. Customers can sell their used fashion items to finance new purchases at partner brands. The items sent to White Stamp are then reintroduced into the market as second-hand goods. To put this proposition in context, the fashion industry is responsible for 8–10% of global carbon emissions, which is more than all international flights and maritime shipping combined.[12]

White Stamp embody the kind of business model that will really make an impact in the European Union's target of bringing an end to fast fashion by 2030. It is also a reminder of fashion designer Orsola de Castro's maxim: 'The most sustainable garment is the one already in your wardrobe.'[13]

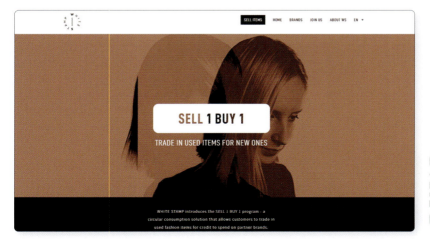

Fig 5.3 Home page for the White Stamp website

Visit the White Stamp website

CASE STUDY

BUSINESS PROFILE: FORESSO

Foresso are an SME based in the UK, producing beautiful furniture, worktops and sheet materials for building interiors using recycled and re-used materials including:

- off-cut timber: only sourced from city maintenance, local sawmills or building sites
- wood dust: used to add a gentle speckle and warmth to the timber terrazzo
- non-toxic and formaldehyde-free binder glue: a unique water-based formulation, developed in-house
- cement and plaster waste: that gives the binder exceptional durability and a fine matt finish.

The company also source all materials from the UK, with an impressive average travel distance of just 43 miles. As well as producing highly circular products, Foresso also prioritise operating an ethical business through how they reward, and invests in employees and are also transparent with business decision-making.

Fig. 5.4 Foresso natural and waste material constituent parts (left to right) binder, off-cut timber and wood dust

Visit the Foresso website

CASE STUDY

BUSINESS PROFILE: PATAGONIA

The American outdoors clothing brand Patagonia are one of the world leaders in sustainable business operations. They don't just produce clothes in a sustainable manner, sustainability is central to who they are and how they operate. In fact, the company, founded by Yvon Chouinard in 1973, received the 2019 UN Champions of the Earth Award for the transformative, positive impact of their business actions on the environment.

There are three key pillars of their global sustainable operations:

Products via the Worn Wear® programme, an online store where customers can purchase second-hand Patagonia products.

Donations via 1% for the planet, which enables companies to donate 1% of their sales to addressing worldwide sustainability issues.

Activism via Action Works, an online portal that allows people to connect to local and regional environmental protection groups.

Patagonia use environmental profit and loss figures to drive decision making about which products to develop, and which to stop making. The company also help supplier chains to reduce their emissions. They are bold and confident enough to admit that their partners rely on fossil fuels, but rather than just telling them to change they are financing energy and carbon audits for those partners that focus on improving energy efficiency, implementing renewable energy off- and on-site and reducing coal and other carbon-intensive fuels used in the manufacture of their products. In addition, Patagonia are heavily invested in regenerative organic farming practices, which help build healthy soil that can draw down more carbon from the atmosphere than conventional methods.

Visit the Patagonia website

Fig 5.5 Sustainable clothing production at Patagonia

CHAPTER 5   ECONOMIC SUSTAINABILITY   117

SME practices and organisations – simply by the fact they make up a large proportion of businesses in the built environment – are well placed to support the uptake and increased visibility of these innovative lower carbon materials. This in turn should help accelerate their widespread use in the marketplace, with the resulting economy of scale cost reductions that occur.

At present, most of these new materials are more expensive than the tried-and-tested, long-standing, typically more carbon-intensive materials our industry is well used to, and which are firmly embedded in supply chain preferred materials and product lists.

This simple comparison of low-embodied carbon, higher cost materials versus high-embodied carbon, lower cost materials raises the question of why we pay more to use more sustainable products.

The 'answer' typically lies in explanations that place the blame for higher prices firmly at the foot of innovation, and expensive research and development processes. Surely Western (and increasingly global) economic development has chosen the wrong path if the burden of achieving and receiving higher economic, social and environmental outcomes is placed solely on those who are willing to deliver or pay for it? The companies producing highly innovative and sustainable products for the good of society and the planet should be incentivised and rewarded for doing so. Those wanting to reciprocate that good through their purchases should not be penalised by having to pay higher prices, fees and taxes. Maybe the carrot and stick approach used to incentivise and disincentivise big corporate companies operating in oil and gas production, for example, should be applied to high-polluting insulation providers.[15]

Manufacturers of sustainable of high-performance insulation should be able to charge affordable prices at a lower level than the more polluting producers. This would encourage mass adoption, rather than leaving sustainable products on the margins, the preserve of those who are the wealthiest or most informed. Such an approach would require significant tax breaks for the sustainable manufacturer, which would also redress research and development investments. Meanwhile, higher polluting manufacturers would be inspired to reform their business models to catch-up, or else leave the game entirely. The ultimate goal here is to ensure that those organisations who remain standing are the most economically viable and sustainable.

It has been suggested that the historical concentration of industry and affluence in developed nations resulted in them bearing responsibility for around 79% of worldwide emissions from 1850 to 2011.[16] Furthermore, it's rational to suppose that those with greater financial reserves often consume more resources. Consequently, it is logical for these countries (namely, the United States, Russia and nations within the European Union and Eurasia) not only to take the lead in global climate initiatives, but also to exceed the efforts of those who haven't reaped comparable financial benefits from contributing to climate change. Considering emissions resulting from consumption, these populations could arguably be the ones needing to make the most significant adjustments in their lifestyles to align with our ambitions for low and zero-carbon outcomes.[17]

However, this is now being challenged/complicated by data suggesting that developing countries are primarily responsible for climate change from 2011 onwards. At the present time, the pendulum has swung, so much so that a significant 63% of annual emissions stem from so-called 'developing nations'. The sectors of industry, energy and prosperity that were historically concentrated in a few advanced countries are now undergoing rapid expansion within developing regions. While this may be a positive development from a societal perspective, this copycat economic view of 'progress' carries a hazardous consequence: namely, heightened carbon emissions.

We appreciate the complex nature of discussions and the range of issues associated with this line of thought, but it would be equally remiss, disruptive and harmful to simplify the debate about how developing regions should develop by arguing they should be allowed to advance with the same carbon intensity as those that have gone before them; as we know two wrongs don't make a right. Today, more so than ever, we are informed about how our prevailing industry. economic and societal actions impact on a global weather systems and the environment, so our socio-political and economic decisions need to be led by this for a greater good, irrespective of geographic location.

> *'Doing "more good" with our commercial ambition, to develop a thriving, circularity-led and resilient business that protects the environment and lifts society.'*
> — Gbolade Design Studio

RE-THINKING BUSINESS ECONOMICS AND ACCOUNTING

There is a perception that quantifying the beneficial economic contribution of sustainable decision making in design and construction outputs is fruitless and challenging. This stems from a belief that there are incalculable aspects of natural ecological elements. Society at large perceives access to nature as a fundamental human right, and thus believes that it should be free. Businesses have treated natural resources in the same way, as unlimited and cost-free.

Discussions about whole-life costing in the built environment have largely focused on the monetary cost of the physical asset in question by way of capital expenditure – its purchase or development, along with maintenance and repair over the course of its lifetime. In recent years, as the conversation has progressed towards more acute considerations of the operational and embodied carbon costs, we need to move the needle even further to consider the wider economic and social implications of our work.

Data exists, and more is being gathered, that supports and evidences the whole-life benefits of long-term, sustainable decision making. SMEs are particularly important in gathering this data. As a set of boots-on-the-ground in the areas they live and work, they can give a true assessment of their socio-economic environment.

As SME architectural practices, when we think about the economics of the built environment, we need to think of it with a regenerative ecosystems frame of mind. We must, in some ways, pull ourselves out of the immediacy of the situation of a project, building or site, and begin connecting the dots of the constituent parts that influence the regenerative development of spaces and places. In doing so, as architects, engineers and built-environment shapers, we can begin to make ourselves critical social actors and shapers. By making the process of systems-thinking at a macroeconomic scale a key part of your small practice's project development process, opportunities for business development strengthen and increase through the ability to partake in wider conversations around projects.

Identifying and understanding systems in local and regional economies can enable architects to operate in more nimble and economically viable ways, while delivering regenerative outcomes for their projects. As small business owners and practitioners, we must develop a business and economic mindset that considers everything. By understanding that all things are connected, and adopting a business model that sees itself as part of a social ecosystem, we can enhance the health of the environment.

This non-linear, or distributive, way of thinking about design, society, the environment and the impact of economic systems must move small practices and architects from a position of not only controlling the design of the buildings, and spaces between the red lines of a site, but also towards a regenerative design systems frame of mind that is wider and more strategic in its considerations. A regenerative approach to design enables long-term thinking that is more of a cyclical, networked approach. At a very basic level, it creates additional multiple revenue streams for small practices as a result of the additional opportunities and visibility that come from a wider range of project stakeholder interactions. More importantly, it also enables small practices to glean insights into existing and emerging socio-economic connections and supply chains being developed, as well as increasing the visibility of the availability and need for complementary resources and facilities for future projects – be it buildings, public spaces or infrastructure. At a more interconnected level, this approach embraces the complexity of socio-economic systems in communities and leverages systems-thinking methodologies to create solutions that not only sustain, but also actively regenerate and improve the health of our environment and communities.

A part of regenerative design is the implementation of circularity in the design and development process. The ReSOLVE framework for a circular economy, developed by global consultancy McKinsey & Company, is a very useful tool that helps businesses to frame their strategies and transition towards this way of project delivery. Moreover, it extends their influence far beyond the red line of a project site and even towards impacting local or national economies.

The framework puts forward six key business principles to action:

1. **Regenerate:** regenerating and restoring natural capital
2. **Share:** maximising asset utilisation
3. **Optimise:** optimising system performance
4. **Loop:** keeping products and materials in cycles, prioritising inner loops
5. **Virtualise:** displacing resource use with virtual use
6. **Exchange:** selecting resources and technology wisely

These approaches can help to fundamentally pivot the approaches taken by small practices such that they understand complex community economic development and social justice issues; bringing these to the forefront of design.[18]

It is crucial to recognise that real change in the world of commerce will only really come to the fore as high-level sustainability calculations and targets filter down to individual companies' accounting.

Towards environmental profit and loss accounting

Puma, a sports footwear and apparel brand that is a subsidiary of the French company Kering (which also includes Gucci, Stella McCartney and Yves Saint Laurent) announced back in 2011 that they would begin issuing an environmental profit and loss (EP&L) statement, which would account for the full economic impact of the brand on the ecosystem.

Other examples of organisations that now use EP&L to guide and drive regenerative economic performance include:

- Phillips: has been using EP&Ls since 2017, building on the use of life-cycle assessment (LCA) methods, introduced in 1990

CHAPTER 5   ECONOMIC SUSTAINABILITY   **121**

– Vodaphone: the first company in mobile phone production to perform a full EP&L
– Novo Nordisk: the first multinational pharmaceutical company to perform an EP&L.

So, what exactly is an EP&L? An environmental profit and loss statement supports a business in measuring the environmental footprint of its operations and across its supply chain, and then calculates the monetary value associated with that footprint.

EP&L statements provide businesses and employees with:

– an understanding of where the environmental impacts are within business workstreams and supply chains
– sound business decision-making processes
– product and process insights relating to sustainable production and procurement
– management of environmental, corporate and health and safety risks
– the ability to compare different types of environmental performance in financial terms.

'Is each product worth the environmental cost? Our environmental profit and loss, or EP&L, metric calculates the carbon, water and waste costs of every item we sell (that goes for our best sellers, too). We use EP&L to drive our product choices; identify and prioritize meaningful improvements; stop making styles until their impact can be lessened; and reduce how much we make. The EP&L holds us accountable to our customers, and the planet.'
— Patagonia

This is a potentially a game-changing metric for all businesses: all businesses understand the need to generate, invest and use financial capital as a key resource. SME architecture practices are no different and should be able to do so too. EP&L accounting helps to bring sustainability front and centre in the minds of business executives, financial decision-makers and investors. It paves the way for

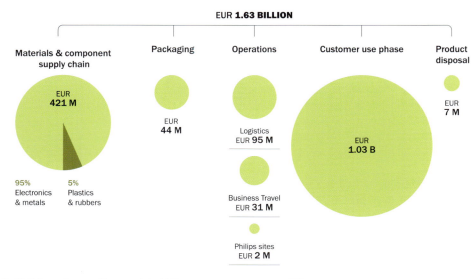

Fig 5.6 Philips environmental impact statistics 2022, source: Koninklijke Philips N.V. 2023

companies to internalise and bring to light costs they might have ignored in the past as externalities.

In the construction sector, we communicate the environmental lifecycle impacts of products with environmental product declarations (EPDs), which are derived from lifecycle assessments. For many non-expert readers, these are still largely unintelligible.

When the cost of sustainable performance is laid out in clear financial terms in an EP&L, highlighting that the environmental damage caused by the business activities exceeds the profits of the company, as illustrated below, it will likely garner greater attention.

How to carry out an environmental profit and loss assessment
Kering, a global luxury brand group, have long been at the forefront of sustainable business improvement. The group has been guided in its business operations through public EP&L reporting since 2012 and has created a digital platform to publicise its EP&L reporting annually.

Kering advises a simple, seven-step methodology for undertaking EP&L accounting:
1. Decide what to measure
2. Map your supply chains (for business and project operations)
3. Identify priority data
4. Collect your primary data
5. Collect secondary data
6. Determine the monetary value of the data

View the Kering EP&L reports

As with some areas of reporting in the world of sustainability and regenerative design, EP&L reporting is very much still developing, so this method of accounting should be looked at contextually within each individual business. In addition, there are challenges around quantifying the financial value of some of the world's natural resources. However, the key here is to focus on readily available and accurate data that you can source or calculate. For SME built-environment businesses, this might be more achievable due to the likelihood of your projects and supply chains being more accessible/local, and the construction environmental product data being more robust than other sectors.

TOWARDS A REGENERATIVE ECONOMIC BUSINESS MODEL: SYSTEMS-THINKING THROUGH THE ECONOMIC BUSINESS CASE

In her widely acclaimed book, *Doughnut Economics*, Kate Raworth presents seven ways to advance our thinking about economics in a manner fit for the 21st century. At a high level, these can help us to generate new ideas for our SME organisations that incorporate the principles of regenerative by design and distributive by design. They may also challenge us to see the world, society and business in completely new ways.[19]

> Raworth's seven ways to re-think economics are:
> 1. Change the goal: from 'GDP and continuous economic growth' to *'the doughnut, thriving in balance'*
> 2. See the big picture: from *'a self-contained market'* to an *'embedded economy'*
> 3. Nurture human nature: from *'rational economic individuals'* to *'social adaptable humans'*
> 4. System savvy: from *'mechanical equilibrium'* to *'dynamic complexity'*
> 5. Design to distribute: from *'growth will even it up again'* to *'distributive by design'*
> 6. Create to regenerate: from *'growth will clean it up again'* to *'regenerative by design'*
> 7. Be agnostic about growth: from *'growth addicted'* to *'growth agnostic'*

Let us consider two of these, which stand out to us as being most interesting from a SME architecture perspective:

Design to distribute: Distributive by design systems are a means of designing economies that are far more value-distributive, sharing value and opportunity more equitably across the whole of society. They lean into the distribution of wealth, from the few to the many, so that the potential to create wealth is placed in the hands of those who might not ordinarily control the land, enterprise or financial institutions.

Create to regenerate: Regenerative by design systems start from a mindset of circularity, re-using, recycling, repairing and restoring. Adopting this approach in our operational and economic activities results in the outputs (products and services) working more in harmony with the earth's resources, improving its restorative equilibrium. The things we make and use from the earth should never be used up but rather re-used over and over again.

These two systems must work in sync with all the other five. But if we consider the boom and bust nature of the construction industry, which is often the first sector to be halted in its tracks by economic downturns, it might be helpful for SME practices to consider how they might operate – and encourage others to do so – in a distributive commercial network of many similar-sized organisations.

At its essence, a distributive by design network consists of many nodes, both small and large, that are interconnected in a web of flows. Through these flows are transfers of energy, resources, people and information. As nature shows us, successful networks reliably and sustainably distribute resources across the whole system. The branched fractals, from small to large, that make up the structure of networks in natural systems, such as rivers and their tributaries, or branches and leaves on trees, support the efficient flow of resources through them, as well as making pathways simple. In addition, the resilience of the whole network is maintained by having diversity and redundancy, which is largely about having a variety of options and routes to take in the event of failure, shock or sudden change.[20]

Applying this systems and distributive thinking directly to construction and architecture, what does nature's inherent resilience teach us about the potential for new economies? If we consider how some sectors within our industry are dominated by large-scale actors – like global practices, tier one contractors or large-scale developer clients – we can see how this can create highly fragile industries, as it squeezes out SME organisations, who make up most of the economy's participants across much of its holistic network. When our industry then suffers from economic recessions and the collapse of some of these large organisations, the implications are widespread and have dramatic consequences on society far beyond those organisations.

DIVISIVE

Capturing opportunity and value
in the hands of a few

DISTRIBUTIVE

Sharing opportunity and value
with all who co-create it

Fig 5.7 From a divisive to a distributive by design ecosystem, adapted from Kate Raworth, *Doughnut Economics*

Wouldn't it be more beneficial to all organisations – small, medium and large – to have a design, construction and built-environment ecosystem that promoted a small-scale fair enterprise system? One that focuses on developing human community and capital from small business in a more equitable manner. One that shares resources and knowledge across multiple similar scale and like-minded businesses in a distributive and reliable way. One that places significant economic value on the small practice, but limits the collateral damage associated from an economic and social perspective when failures occur.

Similarly, with a regenerative by design outlook, we need to prioritise genuine circular economies that are inherently restorative.

'The circular economy refers to an industrial economy that is restorative by intention; aims to rely on renewable energy; minimises, tracks and eliminates the use of toxic chemicals; and eradicates waste through careful design. The term goes beyond the mechanics of production and consumption of goods and services ... (examples include rebuilding capital including social and natural, and the shift from consumer to user). The concept of the circular economy is grounded in the study of non-linear, particularly living systems. A major outcome of taking insights from living systems is the notion of optimising systems rather than components.'
— Ellen MacArthur Foundation[21]

A regenerative architecture, built-environment and construction industry of the future will mimic nature in a way that enables the actors (i.e. your business and the wider supply chain members that make up the industry) to manage waste streams so they are fully recycled in an ongoing circular fashion through value-enhancing economic and social capital flows. These value-enhancing flows are the civic connections that exist between the actors: small businesses, community groups, local religious groups, health centres, schools, local authorities, developers, garden centres and allotments. Through enhanced collaborations between these groups and organisations, across different sectors, cultures and demographics, value can be generated in a sustainable and self-regulating way, and strike an economic balance between efficiency and resilience.[22] Both these ideas of distributive and regenerative by design present opportunities for evolutionary ways of practice, design and engagement for architects, making them central to the regenerative economies of the future.

Transitioning to B Corp Certification: the resilient and social-economically profitable companies of today and tomorrow

In response to these pressing questions and challenges posed by systems thinkers today, one increasing movement in the architecture, engineering and construction sector; is the transition towards certified sustainable business practices, particularly through the global B Corp Movement.

B Corp certification is a designation that shows a business is meeting high standards of verified performance, accountability and transparency on factors from employee benefits and charitable giving to supply chain practices and input materials. Within the architectural community in the UK we are seeing an increase in practices transitioning towards this business model as regenerative and circular economy models have gained prominence. B Corps, with their mission of creating a positive impact, are well-aligned with these sustainability-oriented approaches.

In order to achieve certification, a company must:
– Demonstrate high social and environmental performance by achieving a B Impact Assessment score of 80 or above and pass a risk review.
– Make a legal commitment by changing their corporate governance structure to be accountable

to all stakeholders and achieve benefit corporation status if available in their jurisdiction.
- Exhibit transparency by allowing information about their performance measured against B Lab's standards to be publicly available on their B Corp profile on B Lab's website.

As leaders in the movement for economic systems change, B Corps reap remarkable benefits. They build trust with consumers, communities and suppliers; attract and retain employees; and draw mission-aligned investors. As they are required to undergo the verification process every three years in order to recertify, certified companies are, by definition, also focused on continuous improvement, leading to their long-term resiliency.

For start-ups and micro SME practices in the built environment, this certification process might be daunting. However, there is an intermediate step that you can take in this direction without the full certification commitment at this time. The Pending B Corp status is designed to give start-ups and smaller companies time to prepare for the rigorous process of B Corp certification and comprises a simple three-step process:

1. **Meet the legal accountability requirement for B Corp certification:** The legal accountability requirement means you must incorporate stakeholder governance into the legal structure of your start-up.
2. **Complete and submit a prospective B Impact Assessment:** By completing the B Impact Assessment, you'll learn about B Corp standards and identify the right policies and practices to put in place as your company grows.
3. **Sign the Pending B Corp agreement and pay a one-time fee.**

Fig 5.8 UK B Corp Certified SMEs in the built environment

Visit the Dark Matter Labs

DIVERSIFICATION

To conclude this chapter, we have listed some actions you can take as an SME practice, not only in the pursuit of delivering more sustainable buildings, but also the diversification of your business offering:

- **Promote and undertake diverse/out-of-the-norm activities** to extend the reach and expertise of your practice (see, for example, Arka works in Chapter 3.).

- **Ensure there is awareness among business owners/practice leaders** of the benefits of sustainable and regenerative practice.

- **Encourage and raise awareness among your employees** about the importance of sustainable and regenerative practice; encourage them to explore and research beyond the bounds of architectural design alone.

- **Develop your own environmental profit and loss statement.** Make circular, regenerative and economic performance metrics part of the practice's yearly and half-decade business plan.

- **Invest in capacity-building/training resources to develop holistic sustainability expertise in-house** and assist staff in appreciating positive and negative externalities resulting from project design/development interventions. An example of a negative externality is traffic produced by a building with a lot of parking, where damage is suffered by the neighbourhood, but is not an expense that the private producer paid accordingly. A positive externality would be, for example, the increase in tourism generated by the construction of the Guggenheim Museum in Bilbao, which meant an increase in hotels, sales, restaurants, etc.

- **Invest in developing the knowledge of open-source local and regional data so your practice personnel** can better understand the macro and micro socio-economic temperature, as well as environmental activities. See, for example, London datastore.[23]

- **Diversify the employee discipline pool within your organisation beyond architects.** Our viewpoint stems from considering not only the popularity of emerging roles in architecture, such as computational designers, material scientists, digital designers, generative design and motion graphic designers, but also the potential for integrating social sciences, such as anthropology, economics, political science, psychology and sociology. Going further with this line of thinking, why should SME practices only seek advice and insights from experts in such disciplines in project teams? Shouldn't they have them as employees or at least close collaborators? Examples of leading practices utilising the benefit of such expert insights include Dark Matter Labs, founded by Indy Johar, who is a thought leader in system change, the future of urban infrastructure finance, outcome-based investment, and the future of governance.
Dark Matter Labs is actually a distributed multidisciplinary community of economists, strategists, policy makers, designers and engineers with a shared passion for taking on societal challenges in education, food systems, urban design, logistics, data, policy, finance, healthcare, governance and organisational culture. 3XN/GXN is another such example. While no longer an SME, they are an internationally recognised architecture practice who firmly believe that architecture shapes behaviour, so they've demonstrated that belief through employment/engagement of architects with specialisms in behavioural and cognitive science to shape their strategies and research for the evolution of architectural design.

CONCL

usIon

'Perfection is a stick with which to beat the possible.'
— Rebecca Solnit, writer[1]

We will not pretend that we are there yet: we cannot be. This exploration into the transformative power of regenerative design for small architectural practices reveals a path far surpassing mere sustainability. It is a *journey* towards revitalising our communities, ecosystems and economy. We stress the word journey because we know that while we might have better standards already available to us, true transformation always takes time. It will take us trying, failing, then trying again. And so it should. For *regeneration* comes with the prefix 're', a prefix to which we are so accustomed in our language and perhaps should pay more attention to, for the prefix 're' comes from the Latin meaning 'again' or 'again and again'.

Deeply inspired by the poignant story of Ella Adoo-Kissi-Debrah, this book has hopefully highlighted the profound responsibility of architects in shaping a sustainable and regenerative future. Ella's tragic fate – a direct consequence of environmental neglect – served as a catalyst for the transformative legislation, Ella's Law, emphasising the fundamental human right to clean air. This poignant narrative underscores the critical role of the built environment in our broader ecosystem.

This, and similar legislation, combined with the increasing focus on sustainable standards – such as the UK's Net Zero Carbon Buildings Framework – signals a paradigm shift. Even in the face of changing landscapes, with many practices choosing – as in the case of Sarah Wigglesworth Architects[2] – or else being forced to close down, small practices are still uniquely positioned to champion this shift, transforming ourselves to become generous leaders, moving beyond our comfort zones to empower teams. Embracing the disruption technology has begun to bring and choosing to see that we operate within much larger ecosystems. To make change, we must first – as Tyson Yunkaporta so perfectly summarises in his book *Sand Talk* – respect, connect and reflect.[3]

The journey from traditional sustainable practices to a more dynamic, regenerative approach in architecture marks a pivotal shift in our profession. This transition is not merely an adaptation; it is a revolutionary rethinking of how we, and the buildings we create, interact with the environment and local communities. Regenerative design transcends the conventional objective of minimising harm, aiming instead to actively rehabilitate and enhance our ecosystems.

Furthermore, the integration of advanced technologies, like AI, offers a beacon of hope and efficiency. These tools not only streamline design processes but also open up new avenues for environmentally responsive and sustainable architecture. They empower small practices to compete in a rapidly evolving industry, where innovation is as crucial as resilience.

The role of architects extends beyond design and construction. It involves active advocacy and participation in the environmental movement and in choosing our teams wisely. The power of social media, as shown through influential figures like the intersectional environmentalist Leah Thomas, provides a platform for architects to amplify their voice and impact.[4] As we embrace our role as activists, we also acknowledge our capacity to influence and drive change in policy, perception and practice.

The case studies of the Cuerden Valley Park Visitor Centre and Brattleboro Food Co-op are testament to the transformative power of regenerative practices. By emphasising restorative practices, such as soil regeneration and biodiversity support, and adopting energy-efficient designs, small practices can become catalysts for positive environmental change.

CONCLUSION

Addressing the UK's retrofit challenge presents another significant opportunity. By focusing on regenerative materials and comprehensive retrofit approaches, small practices can improve both environmental and health outcomes. Importantly, the mental health and well-being impacts of building design must not be overlooked. Designs that promote thermal comfort and improved air quality are vital for healthier living spaces.

There is no doubt that the economic landscape for small architecture practices is evolving, necessitating a paradigm shift towards innovative, holistic, regenerative practices. The agility SME architects possess means they can leverage emerging technologies and sustainable practices, contributing to global growth. New economic sustainability measures are gaining importance, urging a transition from resource-intensive approaches. This shift is demanding a reshaping of economics, embracing decentralisation, considering societal and environmental costs and prioritising positive impact.

As SME architects we must promote and incentivise the use and re-use of regenerative products and materials without higher social, economic and environmental costs. The concept of true cost accounting, quantifying hidden expenses and promoting environmentally friendly, yet economically feasible, products must be part of our everyday. The growing trend of EP&L reporting involves measuring the environmental footprint across operations and supply chains and quantifying its monetary value. Whole-life costing offers SMEs an opportunity to play a crucial role in gathering data from local connections and open-source platforms. Meanwhile, adopting a regenerative business and project mindset is an opportunity that allows architects to shape communities through systems thinking. Active community involvement and awareness aligns socio-economic values with project goals.

It is evident that the architecture profession stands at a crossroads. One path leads to continued environmental degradation (albeit trying to slow down the process), while the other promises restoration, rejuvenation and a harmonious coexistence with nature. The choice is clear, and the time to act is now. Our designs, decisions and voices as architects have the potential to forge a sustainable, equitable and thriving future for all. We strongly believe small architectural practices have the potential to be at the forefront of this regenerative revolution. By pioneering regenerative design, we can redefine our built environment landscape, creating a future that is not only sustainable but also thriving and resilient.

Let us step forward with the determination to build not just for today, but for a better tomorrow.

NOTES

PREFACE
1. Lesley Lokko, 'Just City Essays', Just City Lab, 2020 <https://www.designforthejustcity.org/read/essays/lokko> [accessed 6 June 2024].

CHAPTER 1: INTRODUCTION
1. Amanda Gorman, 'An Ode We Owe', Associated Press, 19 September 2022 <https://www.youtube.com/watch?v=ngzY8nJ4-6I> [accessed 19 July 2023].
2. 'See what three degrees of global warming looks like', *The Economist*, 30 October 2021 <https://youtu.be/uynhvHZU0Oo> [accessed 19 July 2022].
3. Candice Howarth, 'One year on from record-breaking 40 degrees heat in the UK and we're still not prepared', London School of Economics, 19 July 2023 <https://www.lse.ac.uk/granthaminstitute/news/one-year-on-from-record-breaking-40-degrees-heat-in-the-uk-and-were-still-not-prepared> [accessed 1 December 2023].
4. Ibid.
5. 'Bringing Embodied Carbon Upfront', World Green Building Council, September 2019, p. 16 <https://worldgbc.s3.eu-west-2.amazonaws.com/wp-content/uploads/2022/09/22123951/WorldGBC_Bringing_Embodied_Carbon_Upfront.pdf> [accessed 21 May 2024].
6. 'Construction statistics, Great Britain: 2022', Office for National Statistics, 19 October 2021 <https://www.ons.gov.uk/businessindustryandtrade/constructionindustry/articles/constructionstatistics/2020> [accessed 21 May 2024].
7. The Fees Bureau, 'RIBA Business Benchmarking: Executive Summary', RIBA, 2023, p.6. <https://www.locarla.com/pdf/RIBA_Benchmarking_2023_Executive_Summary.pdf> [accessed 21 May 2024].
8. 'Worries about Climate Change Great Britain: September to October 2022', Office for National Statistics, 28 October 2022, section 2 <https://www.ons.gov.uk/peoplepopulationandcommunity/wellbeing/articles/worriesaboutclimatechangegreatbritain/septembertooctober2022> [accessed 21 May 2024].
9. Ian Tiseo, 'UK: Construction Industry CO2 Emissions 1990–2019', Statista, 10 August 2023 <https://www.statista.com/statistics/486106/co2-emission-from-the-construction-industry-uk/> [accessed 21 May 2024].
10. '2022 UK Greenhouse Gas emissions, Provisional Figures', Department for Energy Security and Net Zero, 30 March 2023, p. 13 <https://assets.publishing.service.gov.uk/media/6424b8b83d885d000fdade9b/2022_Provisional_emissions_statistics_report.pdf> [accessed 21 May 2024].
11. See Pamela Mang, Ben Haggard and Regenesis, Regenerative Development and Design: A Framework for Evolving Sustainability (Wiley, New Jersey, 2016).

CHAPTER 2: YOUR PRACTICE
1. Mat Braddy in an email to the author, 2024.
2. See Michaela Loach, *It's Not That Radical: Climate Action to Transform Our World* (DK, London, 2023).
3. Alan Moore, *Do/ Build/ How to make and lead a business the world needs* (The Do Book Co., London, 2021), pp. 32–40.
4. Tim O'Callaghan, 'When Will Architects Learn to Value Themselves Properly?', *Architects Journal*, 13 December 2023 <https://www.architectsjournal.co.uk/news/opinion/money-in-architecture-the-value-conundrum> [accessed 6 June 2024].
5. UK Architects Declare Climate and Biodiversity Emergency <https://www.architectsdeclare.com/> [accessed 14 January 2024].
6. 'Net Zero Carbon Buildings: a Framework Definition', UK Green Building Council, April 2019 <https://ukgbc.org/wp-content/uploads/2019/04/Net-Zero-Carbon-Buildings-A-framework-definition.pdf> [accessed 5 October 2023].
7. 'Sustainability Guidance and Checklist', Harlow & Gilston Garden Town, March 2021 <https://hggt.co.uk/wp-content/uploads/2021/10/HGGT-Sustainability-Guidance-and-Checklist-Mar-2021.pdf> [accessed 20 November 2023].
8. See Mike Michalowicz, *The Pumpkin Plan: A Simple Strategy to Grow a Remarkable Business in Any Field* (Portfolio, London, 2012).
9. 'Migrants', Trust for London, 2022 <https://trustforlondon.org.uk/data/populations/migrants/> [accessed 20 July 2023].
10. Ibid.
11. Department for Business, Energy and Industrial Strategy, 'Evidence for the UK Innovation Strategy', Gov.uk <https://www.gov.uk/

government/publications/evidence-for-the-uk-innovation-strategy> [accessed 22 May 2024].
12. Ibid.
13. Philippe Aghion, Antonin Bergeaud, Matthieu Lequien and Marc J. Melitzhion, 'The Heterogeneous Impact of Market Size on Innovation: Evidence from French Firm-Level Exports', National Bureau of Economic Research, revised June 2021 <https://www.nber.org/papers/w24600> [accessed July 2022].
14. See Matthew Syed, *Rebel Ideas: The Power of Diverse Thinking* (John Murray Publishers, London, 2019).
15. V. Hunt, S. Prince, S Dixon-Fyle and L. Yee, 'Delivering through Diversity', McKinsey & Company, January 2018 <http://dln.jaipuria.ac.in:8080/jspui/bitstream/123456789/14237/1/Delivering-through-diversity_full-report.pdf> [accessed 22 May 2024].
16. S. Kumar, R. Ravi, S. Betton and G Leithman, 'When Distinction Disguises Discrimination: A Look at Female and Non-White CEO Performance', Academy of Management: Proceedings, 24 July 2023, no. 1 <https://doi.org/10.5465/amproc.2023.134bp> [accessed 22 May 2024].
17. Simon Aldous, 'News catch-up: Percentage of women architecture students reaches all-time high', RIBA Journal, 12 October 2021 <https://www.ribaj.com/intelligence/news-catch-up-female-students-close-gender-gap-arb-education-michael-gove-concrete-steel-planning-owen-luder-stiff-and-trevillion-tower> [accessed 22 May 2024].
18. Ukuk Bahar, 'Breaking the Bias in Architecture: Gender gap in architecture and construction', Urbanist Architecture, 10 January 2024 <https://urbanistarchitecture.co.uk/gender-gap-architecture/>[accessed 22 May 2024].
19. K. Burnett, 'New data from ARB highlights underrepresented groups in the architects' profession', Architects Registration Board, 12 April 2023 <https://arb.org.uk/new-data-from-arb-highlights-underrepresented-groups-in-the-architects-profession> [accessed 22 May 2024].

CHAPTER 3: ENVIRONMENTAL REGENERATION

1. Etienne Gabel and Francesco d'Avack, 'How will global investments in clean energy evolve to 2030?', S&P Global, 25 May 2023 <https://www.spglobal.com/commodityinsights/en/ci/research-analysis/how-will-global-investments-in-clean-energy-evolve-to-2030.html> [accessed 22 May 2024].
2. 'Heat Pumps', *What They Really Mean for You*, BBC Series 1, episode2, 1 August 2023.
3. See Tom Dollard, *Designed to Perform: An Illustrated Guide to Delivering Energy Efficient Homes* (RIBA Publishing, London, 2019).
4. 'Report of the World Commission on Environment and Development: Our Common Future', United Nations Brundtland Commission, 20 March 1987 <http://www.un-documents.net/our-common-future.pdf> [accessed 22 May 2024].
5. Michael Pawlyn and Sarah Ichioka, *Flourish: Design Paradigms for Our Planetary Emergency* (Triarchy Press, Dorset, 2021).
6. 'The Regenerative Architecture Index', Architecture Today <https://architecturetoday.co.uk/the-regenerative-architecture-index/> [accessed 23 April 2024].
7. V. Masson-Delmotte, P. Zhai, H. O. Pörtner, D. Roberts, J. Skea, P. Shukla, A. Pirani, et al., 'Global warming of 1.5°C An IPCC Special Report on the impacts of global warming of 1.5°C above pre-industrial levels and related global greenhouse gas emission pathways, in the context of strengthening the global response to the threat of climate change, sustainable development, and efforts to eradicate', IPPC, 2018 <https://www.ipcc.ch/site/assets/uploads/sites/2/2019/06/SR15_Full_Report_High_Res.pdf> [accessed 22 May 2024].
8. *Climate Emergency Retrofit Guide*, (LETI, London, 2021), p. 21.
9. The Fees Bureau, 'RIBA Business Benchmarking: Executive Summary', RIBA, 2023 <https://www.locarla.com/pdf/RIBA_Benchmarking_2023_Executive_Summary.pdf> [accessed 21 May 2024].
10. 'Energy efficiency of housing in England and Wales', Office for National Statistics', 2023 <https://www.ons.gov.uk/peoplepopulationandcommunity/housing/articles/energyefficiencyofhousinginenglandandwales/2023> [accessed 23 April 2024].
11. 'Retrofitting social housing: What you need to know', The Housing Finance Corporation <https://www.thfcorp.com/insight/retrofitting-

social-housing-what-you-need-to-know/> [accessed 23 April 2024].
12. Giulia Boselli, 'Housing retrofit challenges and future opportunities explained', Catapult: Connected Places, 19 February 2024 <https://cp.catapult.org.uk/article/housing-retrofit-challenges-and-future-opportunities-explained/> [accessed 24 April 2024].
13. Steph Hazlegreaves, 'Retrofit skills shortage undermines plan to upgrade 19m homes', PBC Today. 18 April 2023 <https://www.pbctoday.co.uk/news/hr-skills-news/retrofit-skills-shortage-undermines-plan-to-upgrade-19m-homes/124849/ [accessed 23 February 2024].
14. 'ADD2678 Retrofit Coordinator funding', London Assembly, 22 November 2023 https://www.london.gov.uk/add2678-retrofit-coordinator-funding [accessed 23 April 2024].
15. 'PAS 2035', Retrofit Academy, 2023 <https://retrofitacademy.org/knowledge/pas-2035/> [accessed 22 May 2024].
16. Ibid.
17. '£1.25bn Announced for Social Housing Decarbonisation Fund Alongside Further Funding for Heat Networks', National Housing Federation, 18 December 2023 <https://www.housing.org.uk/news-and-blogs/news/social-housing-decarbonisation-fund-wave-3/> [accessed 6 June 2024]
18. Becci Taylor and Sean Lockie, 'Retrofit at scale', ARUP, 2024 <https://www.arup.com/markets/cities/retrofit-at-scale> [accessed 22 May 2024].
19. 'Future Trends Survey', RIBA, December 2023 <https://riba-prd-assets.azureedge.net/-/media/GatherContent/Business-Benchmarking/Additional-Documents/RIBA-Future-Trends-Report-December-2023pdf.pdf?rev=699d87005be848e1913ea0d7b1c24550> [accessed 24 April 2024].
20. Alice Lee, Ian Sinha, Tammy Boyce, Jessica Allen and Peter Goldblatt, 'Fuel Poverty, Cold Homes and Health Inequalities in the UK', Institute of Health Equity, 2022 <https://www.instituteofhealthequity.org/resources-reports/fuel-poverty-cold-homes-and-health-inequalities-in-the-uk/read-the-report.pdf> [accessed 22 May 2024].
21. Department for Levelling Up, Housing and Communities, 'Government to deliver Awaab's Law', Gov.UK, 9 February 2023 <https://www.gov.uk/government/news/government-to-deliver-awaabs-law> [accessed 22 May 2024].
22. Alice Lee, et al., 'Fuel Poverty, Cold Homes', op. cit.
23. Ibid.
24. Ibid.
25. Ibid.
26. Ibid.
27. Ibid.
28. Ibid
29. Andrew Burke, 'Condensation, damp and mould – innovative approach to reducing problems', National Housing Maintenance Forum, 24 January 2020 <https://www.nhmf.co.uk/article/condensation-damp-and-mould-innovative-approach-to-reducing-problems> [accessed 6 June 2024].
30. Ibid.
31. Ibid.
32. Sara Edmonds in an interview with the author, 2024.
33. 'Passivhaus Retrofit', Passivhaus Trust, 2023 <https://www.passivhaustrust.org.uk/competitions_and_campaigns/passivhaus-retrofit/> [accessed 22 May 2024].
34. Neal Morris, 'Artificial Intelligence: How are Architects Using AI Right Now and What Are They Using it For?' RIBA, 29 February 2024 <https://www.architecture.com/knowledge-and-resources/knowledge-landing-page/artificial-intelligence-in-architecture> [accessed 22 May 2024].
35. 'RIBA AI Report', RIBA, 2024 <https://riba-prd-assets.azureedge.net/-/media/GatherContent/Business-Benchmarking/Additional-Documents/RIBA-2024-AI-Report.pdf?rev=7fc210b741f3452b9052b701c243b7dd> [accessed 22 May 2024].
36. See Vanessa Nakate, *A Bigger Picture: My Fight to Bring a New African Voice to the Climate Crisis* (One Boat, Basingstoke, 2021).
37. 'Stop and search rate England and Wales by ethnicity 2022', Statista, 5 January 2024 <https://www.statista.com/statistics/284677/police-stop-and-searches-in-england-and-wales-by-ethnicity/> [accessed 22 May 2024].

CHAPTER 4: SOCIAL SUSTAINABILITY AND ENGAGEMENT

1. Toni L. Griffin, Ariella Cohen and David Maddox (eds), The Just City Essays: 26 Visions for Urban Equity, Inclusion and Opportunity, vol. 1 (J. Max Bond Center on Design for the Just City, Spitzer

School of Architecture, City College Of New York, 2022), pp. 1–15.
2. R. Sennett, *Building and Dwelling: Ethics for the City* (Penguin Books, London, 2019), p. 6.
3. See Sebnem Yilmaz Balaman, *Decision-Making for Biomass-Based Production Chains: The Basic Concepts and Methodologies* (Academic Press, 2018).
4. David Peter Stroh, *Systems Thinking for Social Change: A Practical Guide to Solving Complex Problems, Avoiding Unintended Consequences and Achieving Lasting Results* (Chelsea Green Publishing, White River Junction, VT, 2015), pp. 24–8.
5. See A. Bahadorestani, N. Naderpajouh and R. Sadiq, 'Planning for sustainable stakeholder engagement based on the assessment of conflicting interests in projects', *Journal of Cleaner Production*, January 2020, vol. 242 <https://doi.org/10.1016/j.jclepro.2019.118402> [accessed 28 May 2024].
6. Stroh, *Systems Thinking for Social Change*, op. cit.
7. Christina Brook and Louis Schmidt, 'Social Anxiety Disorder: A Review of Environmental Risk Factors', *Neuropsychiatric Disease and Treatment*, February 2008, vol. 4, no. 1, p. 123 <https://doi.org/10.2147/ndt.s1799> [accessed 28 May 2024].
8. Ibid.
9. 'Tours', Los Angeles Eco Village <https://laecovillage.org/home/tours/> [accessed 27 April 2024].
10. 'House of Commons Transport Committee: Investigation into Urban Traffic Congestion', Campaign for Better Transport, December 2016, p. 6 <https://bettertransport.org.uk/wp-content/uploads/legacy-files/research-files/HoC%20Transport%20Committee%20Urban%20congestion%20-%20submission%20from%20CBT.pdf> [accessed 28 May 2024].
11. Stroh, *Systems Thinking for Social Change*, op. cit., pp. 167–94.
12. Ibid., pp. 32–5.
13. Daniel Kim, *Diagnosing Systemic Issues and Designing High-Leverage Interventions* (Pegasus Communications, Inc., Waltham, MA, 2000), p. 2 <https://thesystemsthinker.com/wp-content/uploads/2016/03/Systems-Archetypes-I-TRSA01_pk.pdf> [accessed 28 May 2024].
14. Paula Hooper, Alexandra Kleeman, Nicole Edwards, Julian Bolleter and Sarah Foster 'The Architecture of Mental Health: Identifying the Combination of Apartment Building Design Requirements for Positive Mental Health Outcomes', *The Lancet Regional Health – Western Pacific*, June 2023, vol. 37, np. <https://doi.org/10.1016/j.lanwpc.2023.100807> [accessed 28 May 2024].
15. Kim, *Diagnosing Systemic Issues*, op. cit., p. 7.
16. Nicole Guler, 'Planning Permission Refusal: Top 10 Reasons and How to Avoid Them', *Urbanist Architecture*, 18 January 2024 <https://urbanistarchitecture.co.uk/planning-permission-refusal-top-10-reasons/> [accessed 28 May 2024].
17. Mikaela Loach, *It's Not That Radical* (Dorling Kinersley Ltd, London, 2023), p. 23.
18. 'Regenerative Design Primer', UK Architects Declare, March 2024 <https://www.architectsdeclare.com/uploads/AD-Regenerative-Design-Primer-March-2024.pdf> [accessed 28 May 2024].
19. Ayana Elizabeth Johnson and K. K. Wilkinson, *All We Can Save: Truth, Courage and Solutions for the Climate Crisis* (One World, New York, 2021), pp. xvii–xiv.
20. 'International Women's Day: The Gender Aspects of Energy Poverty', European Parliament, 27 February 2023 <https://www.europarl.europa.eu/topics/en/article/20230224STO76403/international-women-s-day-the-gender-aspects-of-energy-poverty> [accessed 7 May 2024].
21. Johnson and Wilkinson, All We Can Save, op. cit., pp. xvii–xiv.
22. Toni Griffin, 'Defining the Just City Beyond Black and White', The Nature of Cities, 23 October 2015 <https://www.thenatureofcities.com/2015/10/23/defining-the-just-city-beyond-black-and-white/>
23. 'Social Value Toolkit for Architecture', RIBA, May 2020, p. 7 <https://riba-prd-assets.azureedge.net/-/media/GatherContent/Social-Value-Toolkit-for-Architecture/Additional-Documents/RIBAUoR-Social-Value-Toolkit-2020pdf.pdf?rev=8ce05f7e8f7649d09116a13dd3fb9f60> [accessed 29 May 2024].
24. Ibid., p. 6.
25. Ibid., pp. 14–15.
26. See http://www.social-life.co/ [accessed 28 May 2024].
27. 'A Toolkit to Involve Young People in the Making and Managing of Neighbourhoods',

NOTES 137

Voice, Opportunity, Power, <https://voiceopportunitypower.com/> [accessed 29 May 2024].
28. 'Safety in Public Space: Women, Girls and Gender Diverse people', Greater London Authority/Publica, 2022, p. 48 <https://publica.co.uk/projects-gender-inclusion-and-womens-safety/> [accessed 29 May 2025].
29. APPG for UN Women, 'Prevalence and Reporting of Sexual Harassment in UK Public Spaces', UN Women, March 2021 <https://www.unwomenuk.org/site/wp-content/uploads/2021/03/APPG-UN-Women-Sexual-Harassment-Report_Updated.pdf> [accessed 29 May 2024].
30. 'Safety in Public Space', op. cit., p. 17.
31. Ibid., p. 46.
32. See https://www.commonplace.is/ [accessed 28 May 2024].
33. J. Alker, S. Cox, E. Huggett and A. Smith, 'Social Value in New Development: An Introductory Guide for Local Authorities and Development Teams', UK Green Building Council (UKGBC), March 2018, p. 11. <https://www.ukgbc.org/wp-content/uploads/2018/03/Social-Value.pdf> [accessed 29 May 2024].

CHAPTER 5: ECONOMIC SUSTAINABILITY
1. Sanda Ojiambo 'Small Businesses Can Lead the Way to a Sustainable and Inclusive World', World Economics Forum, 8 March 2023 <https://www.weforum.org/agenda/2023/03/small-businesses-sustainable-inclusive-world/> [accessed 1 November 2023].
2. Department for Business, Energy and Industrial Strategy, 'Business population estimates for the UK and regions 2018', Gov.UK, 11 October 2018 <https://assets.publishing.service.gov.uk/government/uploads/system/uploads/attachment_data/file/746599/OFFICIAL_SENSITIVE_-_BPE_2018_-_statistical_release_FINAL_FINAL.pdf> [accessed 30 May 2024].
3. Luke Turner, 'The Role of SMEs in the UK Construction Industry', *Construction Journal*, 24 February 2019, <https://ww3.rics.org/uk/en/journals/construction-journal/the-role-of-smes-in-the-uk-construction-industry.html> [accessed 1 December 2022].
4. 'The Importance of SMEs' Role in Sustainability', Sustainability Knowledge Group, 1 March 2019 <https://sustainabilityknowledgegroup.com/the-importance-of-smes-role-in-sustainability/> [accessed 1 December 2022].
5. See Daniel Susskind and Richard Susskind, *The Future of the Professions: How Technology Will Transform the Work of Human Experts* (Oxford University Press, Oxford, 2015).
6. See Gregory Mankiw, Principles of Economics (9th ed., Cengage Learning, Boston, MA, 2021).
7. J. J. Bish, 'What is Economic Sustainability? Barriers and Inspiration', Population Media Center, 2021 <https://www.populationmedia.org/the-latest/what-is-economic-sustainability> [accessed 1 May 2023].
8. See Daniel Christian Wahl, *Designing Regenerative Cultures* (Triarchy Press, Chicago, IL, 2016).
9. See Kate Raworth, *Doughnut Economics: Seven Ways to Think Like a 21st-Century Economist* (Random House Business, London, 2018).
10. Yvon Chouinard, Jib Ellison and Rick Ridgeway, 'The Sustainable Economy', *Harvard Business Review*, October 2011 <https://hbr.org/2011/10/the-sustainable-economy> [accessed 8 January 2023].
11. Ibid.
12. 'Putting the brakes on fast fashion', United Nations Environment Programme, 12 November 2018 <https://www.unep.org/news-and-stories/story/putting-brakes-fast-fashion> [accessed 1 March 2023].
13. See Orsola de Castro, *Loved Clothes Last: How the Joy of Rewearing and Repairing Your Clothes Can Be a Revolutionary* (Penguin, London, 2021).
14. Environmental Audit Committee, 'Building to Net Zero: Costing Carbon in Construction', UK Parliament, 26 May 2022 <https://publications.parliament.uk/pa/cm5803/cmselect/cmenvaud/103/report.html> [accessed 30 May 2024].
15. 'Carrots and Sticks: How Oil and Gas Companies Are Responding To Energy Transition Policies', Morning Star, 15 August 2023 <https://dbrs.morningstar.com/research/419233/carrots-and-sticks-how-oil-and-gas-companies-are-responding-to-energy-transition-policies> [accessed 30 May 2024].
16. Jonah Busch 'Climate Change and Development in Three Charts', Center for Global Development, 18 August 2015 < https://www.cgdev.org/blog/climate-change-and-development-three-charts> [accessed 30 May 2024].
17. Ibid.

18. See Urban Design Lab <https://urbandesignlab.in/replacing-sustainability-with-regenerative-design/> [accessed 30 May 2024].
19. Raworth, *Doughnut Economics*, op. cit., pp. 26–7.
20. Ibid., p. 175.
21. See Ellen Macarthur Foundation <https://www.ellenmacarthurfoundation.org/videos/explaining-the-circular-economy-rethink-progress?gad_source=1&gclid=CjwKCAjwx-CyBhAqEiwAeOcTdT4G2JMv7xaQ3_uhR9P1FsNjutgSoAGk0QKWHlYmPcx4nv7WicEqyhoC-nMQAvD_BwE> [accessed 30 May 2024].
22. Wahl, Designing Regenerative Cultures, op. cit., pp. 218–19.
23. London datastore <https://data.london.gov.uk/dataset> [accessed 30 May 2024].

CONCLUSION
1. Rebecca Solnit, *Hope in the Dark: Untold Histories, Wild Possibilities* (Haymarket Books, Chicago, IL, 2016), p. 81.
2. Alex Shall, '"A Significant Number of UK Practices Will Fail This Year"', *Architects' Journal*, 8 April 2024 <https://www.architectsjournal.co.uk/news/opinion/a-significant-number-of-uk-practices-will-fail-this-year> [accessed 5 June 2024].
3. See Tyson Yunkaporta, *Sand Talk: How Indigenous Thinking Can Save the World* (HarperOne, San Franciso, CA, 2020).
4. See Leah Thomas, Green Girl Productions <https://leahthomas.com/> [accessed 30 May 2024].

INDEX

Page numbers in **bold** indicate figures and tables.

3XN/GXN 127

activism, environmental 78–79, 130
advanced technologies 68–69, **72**, 73–78, **76–77**, 130
air pollution 10, 42, 130
air source heat pumps (ASHPs) 113, **113**
AirC Digital 74, **74**
Alliance for Sustainable Building Products awards 51
ArchiCAD 68, 69, 73, **73**, 74
Architects Climate Action Network (ACAN) 71
Architects Registration Board (ARB) 37
artificial intelligence (AI) 68–69, **72**, 73–78, **76–77**, 130
Association of Collaborative Design (ACD) 100
augmented reality (AR) 75
Awaab's Law 66

B Corp Certification 125–126, **126**
Better Futures programme 52, 54
bio-based materials 113
Black Females in Architecture (BFA) **36**, 37
Black Lives Matter movement 10, 14, 37, 44
Brattleboro Food Co-op, Vermont 46–47, **47**, 130
Brixton Immortals Dominoes Club 82, **82**, **100**
Brixton Soup Kitchen 82, **82**, 99
Building Regulations 10, 26, 43

carbon emissions 12, **13**, 14, 44, 55, 67, 114, 118
see also embodied carbon
case studies
 AirC Digital 74, **74**
 Brattleboro Food Co-op, Vermont 46–47, **47**, 130
 Collective Works 52–53, **53**

Cuerden Valley Park visitor centre, Preston, Lancashire 51, **51**, 130
Dagenham Heathway 90–92, **90**, **91**, **92**
Foresso 115, **115**
Hill House retrofit 59–64, **59**, **60–61**, **62–63**, **64**, **65**
Knox Bhavan Architects 28–29, **28**, **29**
Los Angeles Eco-Village (LAEV) 86–87, **87**
nimtim architects 23–25, **23**, 24–25
Patagonia 116, **117**
Studio Gil 104, **105**
Studio seARCH 70–71
White Stamp 114, **114**
circular economy **62–63**, 63, 104, 113, 120, 123, 125
Clean Air (Human Rights) Bill 10, 42
client assessment chart 32, **32**
clients, curating 30–34, **32**
Climate Action Venn Diagram 17, **17**
cold homes 66
collaborative approach 33, 34, 49, 54, 93
Collective Works 52–53, **53**
concrete 113, **113**
condensation, damp and mould 56, **57**, 66, 67
construction work, value of 12, **13**
cost–benefit analysis 54
Cove tool 69, 75
Croydon Council 102
Cuerden Valley Park visitor centre, Preston, Lancashire 51, **51**, 130

Dagenham Heathway 90–92, **90**, **91**, **92**
damp and mould 56, **57**, 66, 67
Dark Matter Labs 127
decision-making framework 26–30, **27**, **28**
DesignLCA tool 73, **73**
distributive by design systems 123, **124**
divergent thinking 34–39

diversity 34, 35–37, 70, 94
 see also intersectionality
ecological design trajectory **16**, 45
ecological systems 110
economic sustainability 108–127, 131
 B Corp Certification 125–126, **126**
 case studies 114–116, **114**, **115**, **117**
 diversification 127
 environmental profit and loss (EP&L) accounting 120–122, **121**, 127, 131
 re-defining economics and economic sustainability 109–111, **109**, **111**
 re-evaluating and revaluing 113–119, **113**
 re-thinking business economics and accounting 119–126
 regenerative economic business model 122–125, **124**
 role of small and medium-sized enterprises (SMEs) 108–109, 119, 131
 systems thinking approach 119–120, 122–125, **124**
education and training 33, 34, 49, 54, 127
Ella's Law 10, 42, 130
Ellen MacArthur Foundation 125
embodied carbon 28–29, **29**, **62–63**, 69, 113, **113**, 118
employment practices 24–25
Energy Performance Certificate (EPC) ratings 56, 58
Engagement Overlay to RIBA Plan of Work 100
environmental product declarations (EPDs) 122
environmental profit and loss (EP&L) accounting 120–122, **121**, 127, 131
environmental regeneration 42–54, 68–79, 130
 case studies 46–47, **47**, 51–53, **51**, **53**, 74, **74**, 130

environmental activism 78–79, 130
regenerative approaches 45–54, **45**, **49**
sustainable approaches 43–44, 45
technological tools 68–69, **72**, 73–78, **76–77**, 130
see also retrofitting housing
ethnic and cultural diversity 35–37
Extinction Rebellion 44
extraction economy 22
extreme weather events 12, 44

fashion industry 111, **112**, 114, **114**
Floyd, George 10, 14, 37, 44
Foresso 115, **115**
Formfaktor 73
Future Architects Front (FAF) 25
Future Building Standard 54

Gbolade Design Studio
 Grahame Park project, Barnet, London 66, **101**, **102**
 Hermitage Mews, London **15**
 Hill House retrofit case study 59–64, **59**, **60–61**, **62–63**, **64**, **65**
 'Regenerative Power' installation 82–83, **82**, **83**
 sustainability tools **76–77**
 whole-house retrofit plan **68**
gender diversity 35, 36–37
gender-inclusive urban development 97–99
'Good Growth by Design' programme 97–99
Grahame Park project, Barnet, London 66, **101**, **102**
greenhouse gas emissions *see* carbon emissions
Grenfell Tower 10
gross domestic product (GDP) 110

Harlow & Gilston Garden Town Sustainability Guidance and Checklist 26

Heat Decarbonisation Plans (HDPs) 56
heat pumps 43, 55, **62–63**, 63, 113, **113**
Hermitage Mews, London **15**
Hill House retrofit case study 59–64, **59**, **60–61**, **62–63**, **64**, **65**
Home Energy Action Lab (HEAL) 70

iceberg metaphor 88–89, **89**
Improvement Option Evaluations (IOEs) 56
Innovate UK Building Performance Evaluation study 43
innovation 34–35, 73, 93, 95, 118
Institute of Health Equity 66
internal wall insulation (IWI) 85
International Living Future Institute *see* Living Building Challenge
International WELL Building Institute 50
intersectionality 37, 70, 78, 98

Just Eat 20
just transition and just city 93–95

KBe carbon calculator tool 28–29, **29**
Kering 120, 122
Knox Bhavan Architects 28–29, **28**, **29**
Kyoto Protocol 44

Landscape Institute 100
leadership, regenerative 20–22, **22**, 24–25
Living Building Challenge (LBC) 26, **49**, 50, 54
Lloyd Leon Community Centre, Brixton, London 82–83, **82**
Los Angeles Eco-Village (LAEV) 86–87, **87**
Low Energy Transformation Initiative (LETI) 26, 54, 63
Low Skills Decarbonisation Fund (LSDF) 56

McKinsey & Company 35–36

Marks & Spencer 55
Medium-Term Improvement Plans (MTIPs) 56
mould *see* damp and mould

Net Zero Carbon Buildings Framework 26, 130
Net Zero Carbon (NZC) Building Standard 26, 43
nimtim architects 23–25, **23**, **24–25**
Novo Nordisk 121

objectives and key results (OKRs) 26–30, **27**, **28**
online presence 34
operational energy **62–63**, 69
overheating 67, 69

Paradigm Network 37
Paris Agreement 44
participatory design 91–92, **91**, **92**, 95–104, **96**, **99**, **100**, **101**, **102**, **105**
PAS 2035 56, 58, **58**
Passivhaus 50, 54, 70
Patagonia 116, **117**
pay 24–25, 94
Peabody 67
performance measures 26–30, **27**, **28**
Phillips 120, **121**
pilot projects 54
portfolio building 33
potential-based design 49
Public Sector Decarbonisation Schemes (PSDS) 56
Puma 120
Purley High Street development framework, Croydon, London 102

radical transparency 24–25
recombinant ideas 35
recycled and re-used materials 113, 115, **115**, 123
redundancy 110, 123
Regenerative Architecture Index (RAI) 48
regenerative by design systems 123

INDEX

regenerative design and development 14–16, **16**, 45–54, **45**, 119–120, 130–131
regenerative economic business model 122–125, **124**
regenerative economy 22
regenerative leadership 20–22, **22**, 24–25
'Regenerative Power' installation 82–83, **82**, **83**
regenerative vision 26–30, **27**, **28**
Regenesis Group
    Brattleboro Food Co-op, Vermont 46–47, **47**
    ecological design trajectory **16**, **45**
    Regenerative Practitioner programme 39, 54
renewable energy 43, 50, **62–63**, 64, 78
ReSOLVE framework 120
resource management 93
retrofitting housing 55–67, 131
    case studies 59–64, **59**, **60–61**, **62–63**, **64**, **65**, 70–71
    health and 66–67, 131
    PAS 2035 56, 58, **58**
    retrofit coordinator role 58
    whole-house retrofit approach 67, **68**
RIBA 43
    2023 Climate Challenge 26, 52, 54
    Engagement Overlay 100
    Ethics and Sustainable Development Commission 52
    Social Value Toolkit 95
Royal Institution of Chartered Surveyors (RICS) 26, 43

S&P Global Commodity Insights 43
'Safety in Public Space: Women, Girls and Gender Diverse People' 97–99
Sarah Wigglesworth Architects 130
Section of Architectural Workers (SAW) union 25
'shifting the burden' 85
site visits 33
small practices 14, 20–39
    curating clients 30–34, **32**
    divergent thinking 34–39
    employment practices and pay 24–25
    ethnic and cultural diversity 35–37
    gender diversity 35, 36–37
    objectives and key results (OKRs) 26–30, **27**, **28**
    radical transparency 24–25
    regenerative leadership 20–22, **22**, 24–25
    regenerative vision 26–30, **27**, **28**
    setting targets 26
social housing 16, 56, 58, 66
Social Housing Decarbonisation Fund (SHDF) 56, 58
Social Housing Regulations Bill 66
Social Life 95
social sustainability and engagement 82–105
    case studies 86–87, **87**, 90–92, **90**, **91**, **92**, 104, **105**
    just transition and just city 93–95
    participatory design 91–92, **91**, **92**, 95–104, **96**, **99**, **100**, **101**, **102**, **105**
    social sustainability defined 84
    systems thinking approach 84–93, **89**
Social Value Toolkit 95
Southwyck House, Brixton, London 85
stakeholder engagement 91–92, **91**, **92**, 95–103, **96**, **99**, **100**, **101**, **102**, **105**
steel 113, **113**
stock condition surveys 56
Studio Gil 104, **105**
Studio seARCH 70–71
sustainable design and development 14–16, **16**, 43–44, 45, **45**

Sustainable Traditional Buildings Alliance (STBA) 67
Sustrans 100
systems thinking
    economic sustainability and 119–120, 122–125, **124**
    social sustainability and 84–93, **89**

targets 26
technological tools 68–69, **72**, 73–78, **76–77**, 130
testimonials 33
Thamesmead Estate, London 67
timber 113, **113**
training see education and training
transparency
    B Corp Certification 125, 126
    radical 24–25
    in stakeholder engagement 102
true cost accounting 119, 131

UK Architects Declare 26, 48, 52, 71
UK Green Building Council (UKGBC) 26, 38, **38**, 43, 54, 55
    Future Leaders programme 38–39, **38**, 54
    Net Zero Carbon Buildings Framework 26, 130
United Nations
    Brundtland Commission 44
    Champions of the Earth Award 116
Urban Symbiotics 90–92, **90**, **91**, **92**, 102

value-driven practice 93
Vash Green Schools project, Uganda 78
Venice Biennale 82–83, **82**, **83**
virtual reality (VR) 75
vision, regenerative 26–30, **27**, **28**
Vodaphone 121
'Voice, Opportunity, Power' youth engagement toolkit 96–97

WELL Building Standard 50
White Stamp 114, **114**
whole-house retrofit approach
	67, **68**
Whole Life Carbon Analysis
	(WLCA) 26
whole-life costing 111, 119, 131
whole-system design 49
'Windrush generation' 83
Wolves Lane Centre, Wood Green,
	London 104, **105**
women
	gender diversity 35, 36–37
	pay 94
	safety in public spaces 97–99

Xenophon 109

Zero Carbon Hub inspection 43

IMAGE CREDITS　　　**143**

Fig 1.1 Photograph by Carlos M. Vazquez II, Creative Commons; 1.2 Office for National Statistics; 1.3 Statista; 1.4, 2.6, 3.9, 3.11–18, 3.20, 3.23, 4.1, 4.2, 4.9–14, 5.8 Courtesy of Gbolade Design Studio; 1.5, 3.2 Courtesy of Bill Reed, Regenesis Group; 1.6 Courtesy of Ayana Elizabeth Johnson; 2.1 iStock / Andreyuu; 2.2 Photograph by Marie Jacquemi; 2.3 Courtesy of nimtim, photograph by Megan Taylor; 2.4 Courtesy of nimtim; 2.5 Courtesy of Knox Bhavan; 2.7 Courtesy of Black Females in Architecture, photograph by Tamed Designs; 2.8 Courtesy of UKGBC; 3.1 Ella Roberta Foundation; 3.3, 3.4 Brattleboro; 3.5 Data used published by the International Future Living Institute; 3.6 Courtesy of Cuerden Valley Park; 3.7, 3.8 Collective Works; 3.10 Courtesy of The Retrofit Academy; 3.19 Sustainable Development Foundation / Retrofit-at-Scale / Greg Umiecki / Chris Twinn, 3.21 DesignLCA; 3.22 AirC World; 3.24 Photograph by Verena Berg; 4.3 Courtesy of City Repair; 4.4 From *Systems Thinking for Social Change* by David Stroh (Chelsea Green Publishing, 2015), used here by permission of the publisher; 4.5–4.8 Courtesy of Urban Symbiotics; 4.15 Courtesy of Studio Gil; 5.3 Courtesy of White Stamp, Photograph by Jurica Koletić for Unsplash; 5.4 Foresso; 5.5 Patagonia; 5.6 Based on the data from Koninklijke Philips N.V. 2023; 5.7 Kate Raworth, derived from DEAL doughnuteconomics.org.